BETTER LISTENING

betterlisteningbook@gmail.com

ISBN: 979-8-9884944-0-9 (paperback)
ISBN: 979-8-9884944-1-6 (ebook)
ISBN: 979-8-9884944-2-3 (hardcover)

Library of Congress Control Number: TXu 2-359-101

Printed in the United States of America

Ordering Information:
Special discounts are available on quantity purchases by corporations, associations, and others. For details, contact betterlisteningbook@gmail.com.

BETTER LISTENING

THE SECRET TO IMPROVING YOUR PROFESSIONAL AND PERSONAL LIFE

Stanford Slovin

ACKNOWLEDGMENTS

First, I want to thank my wife and children, who believed in me and allowed me to follow my passion.

I also appreciate all the good advice from my brother and other close relatives, my friends, coworkers, colleagues, and my clients who taught me that I needed to listen better to what they were saying and what was important to them.

I thank my mom who always taught me to be patient and encouraged me to be a better listener.

I also thank my editor, Carol Strubel-Krimm, for guiding me through the writing process, spending countless hours to mold my ideas into a coherent whole, and structuring years of notes into a readable book.

I thank amazing people at Book Launchers who helped me bring this book to life.

Finally, I thank my readers who trust that this book will make them better, stronger, and more empathic listeners.

TABLE OF CONTENTS

PREFACE

To get the most from this book, as you read, find ways to apply the concepts and strategies presented to your everyday life. Use this volume daily as a workbook and a toolchest of practice techniques and best practices.

Challenge yourself to change and adopt some of the techniques shown in the following pages. Make yourself accountable by periodically assessing your progress. Ask yourself, "What could I have done better or differently? What communication mistakes have I made? What improvements have I noticed? What lessons have I learned? What chapters might I benefit by reading again?"

Finally, keep a "listening journal" and jot down your thoughts on the listening process as they occur.

THE PREMISE OF THIS BOOK:

We do not hear what others *really* say because we are not good listeners. We do not let others talk and share what is on their minds.

Our clients, friends, loved ones, coworkers and even passing strangers are all crying out for us to stop talking and *listen*.

Because we don't hear what is being said, we frustrate those who speak to us. They realize that we don't listen to what they have to say or take the time to understand what is important to them. In desperation, some say, "You aren't listening. You don't get it. You are missing the point. Stop talking and *listen* to me!" Sometimes, they turn away with a final, "I'm done since you aren't listening." This happens because all we want to do is proclaim our own opinions.

This book will help you become a better communicator in the professional services industry, any sales role, in any advisory capacity, and in any personal relationship by showing you ways to listen more effectively. This lets others share in a way that strengthens your relationships. You'll be a better advisor because you will more clearly understand your clients and customers. This will produce greater success in the workplace, your personal relationships, and within yourself. This book will help you change your life. Instead of begging to be heard, clients and significant others will say, "You understand what I want to accomplish. You hear me and know what is most important to me. You get me. You know what I am feeling. *You really are listening to **me**!*

INTRODUCTION

How did I end up writing a book on listening?

I am an advisor in financial services, sales, investments, and wealth management. I also have a law degree and have been trained to pursuade, argue, make a case, and tell others what to do. My career has been spent giving advice. Like most advisors, I expected that others would listen to me. That seems obvious but, boy, was I wrong!

My parents repeatedly reminded me that people have two ears and one mouth because they should talk less and listen more, but that idea isn't new. The Greek philosopher Epictetus said, "We have two ears and one mouth so that we can listen twice as much as we speak" all the way back in 60 A.D.

But I didn't take their advice to heart. I felt happy in my wealth management career. My brokerage business was growing, I had a nice clientele and I loved giving advice. I thought I was a good listener since my law school experience helped me quickly identify an issue, understand the rules, analyze the situation, and deliver the solution.

I held that philosophy for my first fifteen years as a financial advisor. My original training included how to sell stocks, bonds, and products my firm offered to investors. In my opinion, the traditional focus of the wealth management and advisory business was sales; and employee training only minimally mentioned allowing clients to share their thoughts about their needs and desires.

Over time, I noticed that I often interrupted and cut off other speakers so I could propound my ideas. I realized that I wasn't listening to others but was, instead, thinking about what I wanted to say next. Occasionally, people would respond, "No, that's not what I meant" or "you don't understand what I'm talking about."

I was sitting in a work conference and the speaker boldly and confidently shared with our group that we were not good listeners. He called us "response mode professionals" who didn't listen or hear what was important to our clients. It hit me right there, fifteen years into my career, that I was doing it *all wrong*. At that very moment, I began a quest to become a more effective listener. I made it my goal to let others (no matter what) empty their bucket *before* I spoke, advised, or responded. I needed to **reflect** (a chapter in this book that will change your whole method of listening).

Before I knew it, conversations became more meaningful, impactful, and fulfilling. Others truly felt and voiced that I had their best interests at heart. I knew I was connecting with them at a much deeper and stronger level.

Listening not only improved my business and allowed me to build an extremely successful wealth management practice, but also improved my relationships with family and friends.

I wrote this book because it was *needed.* Your clients, customers, spouses, children, parents, friends, coworkers, teachers, coaches, and anyone you meet *all want you to be a better listener.* I have spent a decade testing different techniques, principles, and applications of listening skills to identify those that are most effective and produce outstanding results. I share them in the following chapters to help you benefit personally and professionally by becoming a better listener.

So, let's jump in and have fun. I hope you enjoy this book as much as I've enjoyed writing it.

CHAPTER 1

DOES LISTENING REALLY MATTER?

"When people talk, listen completely.
Most people never listen."
Ernest Hemingway

If you're anything like me, you want to make sure that you need something before you buy it, especially any kind of self-help book. So, why is it important to become a better listener?

First, I want to differentiate between hearing acuity and listening. Obviously, humans take in a great deal of auditory information and hearing is a critical part of our five senses. But this book isn't about hearing: it's about *listening*.

Hearing is a physical ability wherein nerves transmit sounds from the ears to the brain.

Listening is a learned skill that occurs within the mind.[1] One must choose to listen to the ideas and perspectives of others, rather than simply hearing them. This is one of the keys to successful leadership because how well a person listens determines how well they connect with and can effectively lead others.

All the great leaders I've studied have been effective listeners. A perfect example of this is Jason Lippert, the CEO of Lippert Components. He is highlighted in *Building the Best* because he takes listening seriously.[2] For example, he holds regular "listening sessions" at the various LCI plants to ensure that his executive team not only knows what his people need but can look for ways to provide it. To quote author Andy Stanley, Lippert's actions are brilliant because, "Leaders who refuse to listen will eventually be surrounded by people with nothing helpful to say."[3]

Think back to your childhood. Do you remember trying to blurt out a comment when the family was sitting around the dining room table? I'll bet your elders hushed you immediately with some version of, "Don't interrupt when others are speaking." You heard similar statements from your elementary teachers like, "You didn't follow instructions. Were you listening?" My favorite was, "If you don't listen, you won't learn." By our teen years, good listening habits should have been ingrained in our minds.

But they weren't. As you became older, think about how many times you said to a parent or significant other, "You don't know how I'm feeling. You just don't get me." And how often they responded, "You talk too much and don't ever listen to me." The value of listening stays the same throughout our lifetime, but we continue to repeat the same listening mistakes as adults that we made as children.

Let's look at a few examples of poor listening. One day, a man preoccupied with his cell phone doesn't pay attention to a neighbor yelling, "Lookout!" As a result, a falling flowerpot cracks him in the head. A college student is daydreaming in class when the professor announces that he is giving the final one day early. She shows up at the original time and discovers that the exam is already over and she has failed the course.

You may feel that you're not like those people. You're a great listener and your clients appreciate your wisdom in providing professional services to guide their needs, so you don't need this book. Take the following quiz and see how good a listener you really are. For the results to be accurate, you must respond honestly. Read each statement, then put an "A" if you feel it is always true about you, an "S" if it is sometimes true and an "N" if it is rarely or never true.

1. I let speakers complete their sentences before I speak. ____

2. I listen to learn the speaker's important points. ____

3. I try to understand the speaker's feelings. ____

4. I attempt to visualize my response before I speak. ____

5. I visualize the solution before speaking. ____

6. I am in control, relaxed, and calm when listening. ____

7. I use listening responses such as, "Yes" and "I see." ____

8. I take notes when someone else is speaking. ____

9. I listen with an open mind. ____

10. I listen even if the other person is not interesting. ____

11. I listen even if the other person is a moron. ____

12. I look directly at the person speaking. ____

13. I am patient when I listen. ____

14. I ask questions to be sure I understand the speaker. ____

15. I do not allow distractions to bother me when I listen. ____

16. I make sure I understand the other person's point
of view before I respond. ____

Once you've finished, count only your "A" responses.

14 - 16 You are an excellent listener.

11 - 13 You're a good listener but could use help in a few
areas.

7 - 10 You are a fair listener.

4 - 6 You are a poor listener.

0 - 3 You are a very poor listener who needs to brush up
on active listening skills.

Even if you didn't score well, you may feel that those
in advisory roles don't really need to listen to their cli-

ents. We don't have time to hear all the details of their lives and we are the experts who possess the knowledge. Customers are supposed to listen to the wisdom of their advisors. Right? *Wrong!* Being in this industry for over thirty years, what is evident is that poor communication is the most common reason clients leave advisors. The clients feel that advisors never ask what's important to them, don't listen to their views or understand what they want to accomplish, don't have their best interests at heart, and are out only for themselves. Rather than being open-minded, they find that advisors are overly quick to respond, condescending, controlling, and don't let them share what is really bothering them.

These results make it clear that customers expect prompt follow-up when they have questions or concerns. They want to be heard and are hungry for thriving, open communication beyond advice-giving, reports, and reviews. Clients want their advisor to be supportive of their needs, wants, and life goals.

People who feel that they are smarter than their audience may not respect the views of other speakers. As advisors, we think customers should agree with our point of view. But that may not be what our clients want. When they realize you are not listening, they turn you off. People don't like being talked at. It frustrates and upsets them when you don't value their opinions or understand that they want to share something with you. Your advisor agenda is getting in the way of building lasting relationships with your customers.

Because better listeners tend to have stronger, deeper relationships with others, becoming a better listener will improve your client relationships and your bottom line.

Therefore, I want you to accept my challenge and take the pledge: "I (insert your name), do solemnly swear to be a good listener and try to listen more. I will use this book to learn ways to become a better listener."

CHAPTER 2

WHY ADVISORS (AND OTHERS) DON'T LISTEN

"Most people do not listen with the intent to understand; they listen with the intent to reply."
Stephen Covey[4]

If listening is so important, why are most people such poor listeners? Given all the conversations we have every day, you'd think we'd all be great listeners but most of us are not. We hear others but don't actively listen; and that's a big difference. Let's examine the main reasons.

When sitting in face-to-face conversations with friends, children, spouses, partners, or work colleagues, how frequently do you think about nothing else other than the words that are coming from their mouths? Probably not too often. And you are not alone. Research indicates that people focus on formulating their responses rather than listening to comprehend what others are saying over 90% of the time.[5]

We often *believe* that we are listening but we're actually only considering how to jump in to tell our own story, offer advice, or even make a judgment - in other words, not listening to *understand*, but to *respond*. Active listening means that you are in the conversation to

understand the point of view and the perspective of the other person. This is called *being in their operating reality*.[6] It does not mean you are preparing to respond.

Think about your own business and personal conversations. Review how often you plan your next response before the speaker has finished or say things like, "Yeah, I get it but" or "Let me explain it to you." When we don't listen to others, we cannot understand their needs. This causes misunderstandings, frustration, disagreements, silence, non-sharing, a lack of trust, and eventually a *complete communications breakdown.*

Despite the reality that it is far more effective to listen contentedly to someone's entire thought rather than to wait impatiently for a chance to respond, leadership expert and coach Marcel Schwantes says that we often treat communication as if it were a race with the goal to have no time gap between the conclusion of another person's sentence and the beginning of our reply. It takes an enormous amount of energy and is incredibly stressful to sit at the edge of your seat trying to guess what the person in front of you (or on the telephone) is going to say so that you can fire back a response. Listening to understand eases that tension, makes other speakers feel more relaxed, and increases their responses because they don't have to compete for "airtime" (Schwantes).[7]

> As busy, distracted professionals, we have a million things on our minds and have mastered the art of simultaneously talking on the phone, responding to emails, updating CRM, and sending texts. We also multitask while others speak rather than focusing on their content. We are so distracted by dings and tweets from our smartphones that we struggle to listen when people talk to us.

The many digital gadgets in our lives have made us more productive, but less attentive and focused on single details. Our minds wander to other concerns because we are not accustomed to really listening. Many studies have confirmed this high level of distractibility and poor recall.

One experiment in Minnesota asked students to summarize the topic after their teachers stopped in mid-lecture. Correct responses fell from 90% at the first-grade level, to 44% in middle school and 25% in high school (Sullivan and Thomas).[8]

We listen even less effectively as we age. Only about 10% of adults are effective listeners, due mostly to environmental distractions. The human brain itself is partly responsible for the problem. Because it can process up to 400 words per minute and most speakers talk at under 125 words, three-quarters of your brain is looking for something else to do while someone is speaking with you (Sullivan and Thompson). You might start out legitimately trying to pay attention but quickly become distracted by other sights and sounds around you. A perfect example is attempting to have a conversation with the television on in the background. While someone is speaking to you, your eyes and ears stray to that sports event, movie, or even commercial on the tube and miss what the speaker is saying.

They may feel momentarily hurt that the television is more important than what they are saying, but they can always repeat themselves. Inattention may sometimes have much more serious consequences. The National Safety Council estimates that distracted driving due to cell phone use and texting causes 1.6 million accidents yearly (El).[9]

Many advisors believe clients cannot speak logically about their own needs because they have limited experience or expertise. Since there is nothing important to learn, conversing with customers is simply a waste of their valuable time; and they only grudgingly listen to clients as a favor to superiors. (Will you please listen to him? He has a problem.).

Instead, these advisors feel they must "spread the word and wisdom" by telling clients what to do. As a bonus (although it does nothing for customers), this highlights their own abilities and intelligence, as well as stroking their egos and feelings of superiority.

We are so self-absorbed and focused on our own lives and feelings that we often forget to maintain attentive concern to the wants and needs of others. Therefore, we lack the patience, compassion, and empathy necessary to listen effectively. Prideful, overbearing and controlling personalities often thwart our efforts to be good listeners.

We have not specifically learned how to be good listeners.

We have preconceived notions that the speaker talks endlessly or is not interesting.

We are protective of our views, become defensive, and tune out others who are critical or tough on us.

Howard Gardner, author of *Changing Minds*, has examined the research and summarized his findings into four main causes of "bad listening:"

- A lack of respect for the speaker.
- Being trapped in one's own head by one's thoughts.
- Hearing only superficialities and missing the real meaning.
- A general ignorance of social politeness.[10]

Let's be clear. I am not questioning the reality that advisors still need to guide and help our customers. We must provide solutions, insight, direction, and advice. But *first*, we must help clients communicate to their advisors what is important to them and then really listen to what is on their minds. This holds true for any person in a sales capacity and for all professional service providers: financial advisors, attorneys, accountants, insurance agents, bankers, and real estate representatives, to name only a few.

CHAPTER 3

SIGNS OF POOR LISTENING

*"When you talk, you are only repeating
what you already know but if you listen,
you may learn something new."*
Dalai Lama

Most of us talk to ourselves. Think about the last time you did. Did you cut yourself off, interrupt yourself, tune yourself out or stop yourself from saying something? Of course not. Instead, you thought through a situation and resolved it by talking, listening to what you heard, understanding your thoughts and feelings; and then talking and responding over and over until you had a handle on the issue.

We never interrupt ourselves, yet we cut off others all the time. Our clients, family and friends are frustrated when we don't listen and talk *at* them rather than *with* them. So, how can we change?

The first step is to recognize the clear signs that we are not listening. We must identify and eliminate our ineffective, *high-risk* listening responses. These statements take the focus off the speaker, block genuine communication, and generate negative feelings. They lower the speaker's self-esteem and lessen both their motivation to share and the initiative to solve their own problems. Others feel blocked from communicating in depth because our high-risk responses imply that we want to change or modify them (Katz and McNulty).[11]

HIGH-RISK RESPONSES

We hijack the conversation and "talk over" others.

When someone starts to share a situation, problem, or issue, we immediately stop listening and interrupt with comments or advice. This inhibits others from voicing their opinions, concerns, or problems, and sends the message, "I'll tell you since you're too dumb to figure this out."

Interrupting is **the** cardinal sin of conversation. Think about your own experiences. It's upsetting when you begin a story or try to make a point and someone else jumps in before you are finished. I remember being in a group of people and giving up trying to add anything to the conversation. Everyone was so intent on making their own point that as soon as someone else finished, or even before, they would jump in with what they wanted to say without a pause. I finally gave up. I didn't want to try to compete with people who had no interest in my input because they were so focused on being the next to talk.

To take enough time to listen to people, implement the two-second rule: wait two full seconds *after* someone talks before you speak. This ensures that they are finished and demonstrates that you were listening and are thinking about what they are saying.

We hear a problem and immediately leap in to tell others what to do.

This shifts the focus of the conversation from the speaker's concerns to our own diagnosis and judgment of their issues. Such evaluations tell others, "There's something the matter with you that I can fix."

Everyone has experienced situations where someone simply wants to share, but we are not good at recognizing the signs. You come home and your loved one tries to tell you about a problem with a friend, an issue at work, or a challenge with a family member. They begin explaining the situation and try to share what is happening and bothering them. Suddenly, you transform into the "super solver." The gears in your mind whir, "solving" juices flood through your body, and your mouth tingles with the answer. You can't wait to come to the rescue, and quickly blurt out the perfect solution. To your surprise, you hear, "All I wanted was for you to listen to what happened, not to give me your solution."

It's easy to interrupt and announce what we think others should do. Unfortunately, others are often not looking for advice, but only want someone to listen to them. Instead of voicing your opinion, dig deeper into the issue and ask the speaker to tell you more. Learn about how they feel. In doing so, you may even help them figure out a solution on their own.

If others want advice, they'll tell you. If you aren't sure, just ask, "Do you want me to listen or would you like my input?"

People don't share with you so that you can point out what they did wrong or should have done better. There may be a place and time for that, but most speakers just want you to listen.

We ignore the importance of other's experiences.

Often, when someone tells us a personal story, it triggers the memory of a similar incident in our life, and we interject to describe it. However, telling our story isn't being empathic — it takes the focus off the speaker and puts it on us.

If you want to be a good listener, rather than interrupting with your own narrative, ask the speaker more about theirs. Dig deeper and probe into their experience. Ask them to expound on it. This will show that you are really interested and will help to create a stronger connection with them. Of course, you may also share your own stories, but don't rush it. Focus on the speaker before adding your own experiences. If you are in a conversation about the good time a speaker had at a local restaurant, don't interrupt with, "I was there last week, and this is what happened to me." If a client tries to share memories of a favorite vacation, don't cut in with your own story and prevent them from sharing their memories.

We derail the speaker's agenda with pat reassurances that "everything will be all right" and change the subject.

A speaker might be talking about a sensitive issue or a topic that is meaningful to them. Because the subject makes you nervous, you aren't interested, or you think you have better content to deliver, you steer the conversation to something that interests you more or that makes you feel safer. This inhibits the speaker from broaching the subject again.

Even when we let others speak, we don't ask questions or paraphrase what we've heard.

When a speaker tries to share, we often use short, meaningless responses such as, "I agree" or "that's nice" which lead to extremely limited dialogue and often shorten, finish, or diminish a potentially engaging, deeper and meaningful talk.

I remember a time I was listening to a client rambling on about his WWII service. I nodded, smiled and when he'd finished, responded with, "Wow, that's great." The conversation ended abruptly, and I realized I'd blown it. I knew there was something missing, so I quickly regrouped and added, "It sounds like your service was incredible and formed an important part of your life. Tell me more about your most moving and unforgettable memory."

He stood tall with a smile on his face and continued in a strong, brave voice to talk about his tour of duty and his role in saving fellow servicemen by landing on makeshift airfields with supplies and taking the wounded back to safe Allied areas. I never would have heard that story or shared that meaningful moment had I not changed my way of listening and reflecting.

Rid yourself of your internal filters.

Our brain is amazing. It remembers feelings, things, and experiences to make learning faster and easier. The problem is that unless we are intentional about actively listening, we allow our brains to take over and apply filters from the past that distort our ability to listen. For example, salespeople who hear the same objection multiple times begin to assume that everyone has the same reason for giving that objection. Consequently, they don't ask questions to try to understand why, but simply give their standard response.

Negative body language reveals that we are poor listeners.

We don't look like we are paying attention if we slouch or turn away from a conversation. Always position yourself to fully face the speaker. If your feet are angled away, it gives the impression that you want to leave. Lean forward and nod or smile occasionally to give the speaker positive feedback.

I frequently spot people at parties, networking events, and even weddings that approach and greet someone, then begin looking around at others while that person is attempting to respond or converse with them. Not only is this rude and inconsiderate, but it is clear evidence of poor listening.

To show that you are listening, look the speaker in the eye. You can move your glance from one eye to the other if this feels too direct. Avoid looking at your phone, other people in the area or toward other conversations. This shows a lack of interest and makes others feel unimportant.

To really show that you are interested in what a person has to say is to truly *be* interested. If you do that, the body language will follow. If you try to fake it by doing the "right" moves, that will also be apparent.

We take things personally - the Defense / Response Mode.

Have you ever had a relationship with someone who waits for you to say something slightly off or not to their liking, and then immediately jumps at that statement and criticizes that one comment, or, even worse, corrects you in a superior fashion? I refer to that as *looking to attack the flaw.* You can say five hundred things in a conversation but if you get a single fact, word, or phrase wrong, the person stops listening and gets aggravated, defensive, or judgmental. Such people use sarcasm, "jokes," and anger to derail any hint that they should change something about themselves or the way they do something.

Especially when we have a close relationship with someone, it is easy to take what they say personally and get defensive but that's counterproductive. When we start defending ourselves, we no longer hear what the other person is trying to say, and frequently attack them instead of focusing on the matter at hand.

This usually makes matters worse. People *never* want to hear hostile responses like, "You don't know what you're talking about," "that's a dumb thing to say," "you are clueless – you just don't understand," or "you're talking like an idiot." Attacking as a first response is an immediate warning flag. It puts others on the defensive or in shutdown mode because you made them feel inadequate and worthless.

If you are the listener, try not to get defensive. Hold your tongue. Just listen to what the speaker is trying to say and attempt to figure out why they are saying it. If you believe their motives are negative, remove yourself before responding. Rather than threats such as, "You'd better not say that," tell the speaker that you need time to think about the issue and calm down before continuing the conversation.

Attacking a speaker never helps your relationship but listening to them and acknowledging their viewpoint is not the same thing as agreeing with it. You may disagree with their assessment. If you explain your perspective without making negative comments, you will have a much greater chance of better understanding and maintaining a positive relationship.

If you recognize yourself in any of the above scenarios, it's time to make some changes. Poor listening has a negative effect on your work, your friendships, and your personal life. It's worth putting forth the effort to become a better listener.

CHAPTER 4

RESULTS OF POOR LISTENING

*"Please listen, and just hear. And if you want to talk,
wait a minute for your turn – and I will listen to you."*
Leo Buscaglia

RESULTS OF POOR LISTENING

People turn you off when you don't listen, or never get to the deeper issues because you interrupted them. Conversations should be well balanced, with all parties getting equal time to speak. Monopolizing a conversation prevents you from listening and others from fully expressing what they want to say (Doyle).[12]

Responding in a way that fails to answer the question also reflects poorly on your listening skills and will lead to you making a poor impression, especially in a job interview (Doyle).[13]

After an introductory meeting or visit with a potential new client, I always ask myself, *Did I do most of the talking or more of the listening? Did others truly get to share what was on their minds, or did I spend too much time talking about myself and my agenda?*

Distractions in the environment also increase customer dissatisfaction. How many times have you texted while someone else is speaking, surreptitiously glanced at your phone to not miss something important, or stared blankly at the speaker with a bored expression? When you multitask, you aren't paying attention to the conversation at hand. This violates our most treasured human ability — communication.

Due to the complexities of business, however, it may be impossible to ignore vital communications from others during meetings or presentations. The simple solution is to apologize before the conversation and inform the speaker that you may be forced to temporarily pause and take a critical call or respond to a text during your meeting. This not only shows consideration and respect for the speaker, but their response allows you to gauge their degree of acceptance for such interruptions.

We completely disrespect others when we don't listen to what they have to say. This is unpleasant and frustrating for them. What if you were the person who was cut off and whose concerns weren't heard? How would you feel?

When we shut others out, they eventually become silent, and our relationship with them is damaged.

TIPS TO IMPROVE

- Show the speaker that you are paying attention by not talking. Hold your comments and listen.
- If you catch yourself not listening, don't hesitate. Ask the talker, "I know what you are saying but please explain it again, so I don't miss anything.
- Watch and copy good listeners. Learn from someone who you feel is a good listener and steal their method.
- Maintain eye contact with the speaker but relax your gaze. Don't strain your eyes or over-concentrate but focus on the speaker in a natural, unforced way (Osten).[14]
- Use your body to show interest. Nod occasionally, get on the edge of your seat and lean toward the speaker.
- Ask a friend or colleague to coach you by watching and critiquing as you listen.

- Go back to the speaker and check to make sure you have heard what they were trying to share with you.
- Block distractions like surrounding sounds and activities that might distract you.
- If a speaker's speech pattern or accent starts to catch your attention, bring your focus back to the words themselves.

CHAPTER 5

ACTIVE LISTENING – ATTENDING

*"Listening is an art that requires attention over
talent, spirit over ego, others over self."*
Dean Jackson

The best way to exceed the expectations of others is to become an active listener. This ensures that no information is lost, and the concerns of others are not simply taken for granted or ignored.

Active listening begins with the conscious decision to totally concentrate on what is being said and understand the messages of the speaker. The process improves personal relationships, reduces misunderstandings, and strengthens cooperation. It requires that the listener attend, understand, respond, and then remember what is being said.[15] Active listening involves the skills of attending, reflecting, and clarifying. This chapter discusses methods to enhance attending skills.

ATTENDING SKILLS

Attending means giving physical and psychological attention to another person in a communication situation that demonstrates nonverbally to the speaker that the listener is interested and paying careful attention.

Physical attending occurs when a listener adopts an involved posture that includes facing the speaker, establishing good eye contact, avoiding distractions, maintaining an interested silence, and arranging to have an appropriate environment for the conversation (Katz and McNulty).[16]

To be effective listeners, people must spend their energy processing and focusing on what they are hearing and learn to resist the many distractions of all shapes and sizes that cross their paths. Distractions and noise come in two broad types, internal and external ("Enhancing").

External distractions are noises or images in the physical environment. Loud noises and unnecessary or excessive images can both inhibit effective listening. For example, think how difficult it would be to have a meaningful conversation with a friend while someone else is having a loud argument in the same room. To focus most effectively on a speaker's message, remove all the distractions possible. Turn off mobile devices, relocate to a quiet space, and close unnecessary computer windows ("Enhancing").

Internal distractions refer to psychological and emotional "noise." Hunger, distress, or physical discomfort can be just as detrimental to effective listening as things in the environment ("Enhancing"). If a speaker is nervous, for example, he or she may be distracted by a litany of negative thoughts from that "little voice" in the mind. Internal distractions can also occur when a listener is thinking about later plans or topics completely unrelated to the conversation at hand.

Listening requires the conscious attempt to decode and interpret both verbal messages and nonverbal cues like tone of voice, facial expression, and physical posture. Therefore, to develop the most accurate understanding of the speaker's message, active listening also involves observing and parroting the speaker's behavior and body language. This is especially important with international communications because various cultures have different expectations about appropriate positions and distance during conversation. If one attending behavior doesn't seem comfortable for the speaker, try another.

For example, if the speaker wants face-to-face dialogue with full eye contact, do that. If sitting side-by-side seems more comfortable for the speaker, do that instead.

When a listener does not react to a speaker's nonverbal cues, he or she engages in a content-only response that ignores the emotions that guide the message and limits understanding.

ATTENDING COMPONENTS

Contact

Eye contact is one way of indicating interest, as the eyes are a key communication mode. This does not mean that eye contact should be a fixed stare. If you are honestly interested and at ease, you'll look naturally at the other person throughout a conversation.

Distance

Another element of attending is the distance between the speaker and listener. It is important to base this on the comfort level of the other person. I remember a few instances at work events and with friends where someone made me uncomfortable by violating my personal space. It was almost like they had to be standing only inches away to get their point across. I quickly ended the discussion to escape the "get out of my face" feeling.

Some experimentation is usually necessary before two people discover the most comfortable distance between themselves.

Gestures

We communicate a great deal through body movements. If you fidget, drum your fingers, cross your arms, or sneak glances at your watch while listening, you may be sending an unintended message to the speaker (Katz and McNulty).[17] It is vital to use only gestures that are consistent with what is being communicated.

Environment

The environment, or setting, should support communication and promote privacy. In conversations, remove barriers between yourself and the speaker such as a large table between you, an open car door, or a crowded location (Katz and McNulty). If that is impossible, consider choosing an alternate space or a more appropriate time to communicate.

Interested Silence

A period of active, attentive silence serves as a gentle nudge to another person to move deeper into a conversation. It allows them time to think and reflect and then proceed at a comfortable pace. If the speaker pauses, the listener can maintain interest without saying anything.

"Giving the speaker time to experience and explore the feelings that churn up from within often enables him or her to explore their feelings at a deeper level" (Katz and McNulty).

Silence is especially useful in situations of loss or grief, such as the death of a loved one or other significant personal loss. Appropriate silence is also useful in helping another person talk about a difficult problem.

According to life and career coach, Caren Osten, most of us are uncomfortable with pauses. Rather than considering them awkward silences, use these times to reflect on the meaning of what a person has just said. Try to keep your mind from wandering during such moments of silence; there may be significance behind the pause itself (Osten).[18]

Try to embrace silence and listen to both words and the silence between them. Allow speakers to finish each point before asking questions or responding ("Empathic"). Let a pause between their sentences sit for a few seconds in case the speaker has more to add.

The primary message sent by attending is that the speaker's physical presence and what he or she says is important. Active listeners should adjust the intensity of their attending behaviors to the speaker's level of comfort and keep the focus on the speaker. As the first step in the active listening process, *attending* allows the listener to hear and understand what the speaker is communicating through words and body language.

CHAPTER 6

ACTIVE LISTENING – REFLECTING AND CLARIFYING

*"I think one lesson I have learned is that there
is no substitute for paying attention."*
Diane Sawyer

In addition to attending, active listening also requires *reflecting,* the process by which a listener restates or paraphrases the thoughts and feelings learned from a speaker's words, tone, body posture and gestures back to the speaker (Katz and McNulty).[19] Reflection is a crucial part of the listening process. It starts *right at the beginning* of the exchange with the speaker and is the *most* important "crossroads" of a successful conversation or a failure to listen effectively.

REFLECTIVE LISTENING WORKS IN MANY SITUATIONS

- To help another person with a difficulty or problem.
- During conflict management and negotiations.
- To create a climate of warmth between people.
- To minimize the resistance or anger of others.
- To effectively lead group discussions.
- To ensure directions are correctly understood.
- Whenever a speaker has a strong need to be heard.
- To ease listener confusion about a speaker's statements.

OVERVIEW

Reflecting involves paying respectful attention to the content and feelings expressed in another person's speech about their needs or problems, understanding that communication, and then letting the speaker know that he or she has been heard and understood. This makes the speaker feel important, comfortable, and appreciative. It requires that listeners keep their attention focused completely on the speaker without offering their own perspective (Katz and McNulty).[20]

During the conversation, the listener checks in periodically with the speaker and uses reflecting and clarifying to allow all participants to understand both the feelings and content of the communication. It would not make sense, nor would it be a meaningful conversation if both sides were not hearing the same message.

Reflecting confirms what the listener heard, helps both parties understand each other, and assists the listener to better retain that information for future access. Reflections might include comments like, "I heard you say but I just want to make sure I am clear on that," or "I heard you say... Tell me a little more about that." It is important to remember, however, that simply paraphrasing a speaker's message does not indicate that you necessarily agree with the speaker ("Enhancing").

These reflections or restatements provide a check to verify that the listener accurately understands what the speaker is communicating. If the speaker hears a reflection that fits their current model of the world, he or she continues the conversation without a break. If the reflection is slightly off target, the speaker becomes aware of the mismatch and makes the necessary correction. For example, a speaker may respond, "No, that's not quite right. I think it's more like irritation." A reflection that is completely inaccurate derails the conversation and forces the focus away from the speaker (Katz and McNulty).[21]

Reflective listening requires that listeners interrupt the speaker's narrative to reflect his or her communication. Some people speak so quickly that this is difficult to do.

However, if the listener doesn't reflect, speakers may begin to repeat themselves or become frustrated because they don't feel the listener understands.

On the other hand, accurate reflections promote continued conversation (Katz and McNulty).[22]

For the process to be effective, listeners must be able to accurately comprehend the speaker's communication at both the content and feeling level; and then make frequent, short reflections of small conversational segments in their own words. Each of these may capture a thought, feeling, or meaning; or several might fit together under a theme or in some other specific way.

Reflecting such small chunks allows the listener to digest a workable amount of content and feelings and lets both parties focus their cognitive abilities on a manageable segment of a whole communication (Katz and McNulty).[23]

LISTENER STEPS IN THE REFLECTION PROCESS

1. **Take in Cues** – As a speaker communicates, identify and record cues in three areas:
   Content - The actual words spoken and their meanings.
   Feelings - Implied or stated feelings or emotions.

Context - Material the listener knows that relates to but isn't expressly communicated during the conversation.

2. **Acknowledgments** – Brief, one to three-word statements or nonverbal gestures that show the speaker that the listener comprehends and is following the conversation.

3. **Sort** – Sift through the cues to determine the essence of a particular "chunk" of the communication.

4. **Draw a conclusion** – Mentally formulate a sentence about what the speaker is trying to say.

5. **Express the essence** – Reflect the conclusion to the speaker to verify listener understanding of what the speaker said.

DETAILS OF THE REFLECTIONS PROCESS

Reflecting content requires the listener to focus on a speaker's thoughts, ideas, beliefs, facts, and data during a particular communication; then rephrase the essence of a segment of that communication to the speaker.

The process enables listeners to check their understanding of content-centered communications, directions, plans and agreements; confirm they are answering the correct question in group discussions; facilitate problem-solving; manage conflicts to understand another person's position, interests, and values; and give feedback on how well a speaker is communicating. In addition, when a speaker is either communicating rapidly or conveying a lot of information, listeners can take a short "mental vacation" before refocusing and checking back with the speaker. Reflecting content also helps speakers gain direction, work toward resolving a given concern or problem, and reduce unnecessary repetition (Katz and McNulty).[24]

Reflecting feelings involves listening accurately and using a "feeling" word to express the essential emotions stated or implied by the speaker. This makes both the speaker and listener more clearly aware of vaguely expressed or hidden emotions and assists speakers to "own" or express their feelings. Speakers often generalize about their emotions as if such feelings were not part of themselves, but feelings are frequently even more important than content in communication. There is great value in identifying both negative and positive feelings, and reflective listening allows the listener to participate in this process.

Reflecting feelings depends on a listener's ability to identify them. Strong emotions like love, hate, disgust, fear, or anger are typically easy to recognize. More subtle feelings such as affection, pleasure, hostility, guilt, or anxiety, however, are often disguised behind non-feeling words. A listener can help identify such hidden feelings by carefully watching both the speaker's physical (energy, body position, and facial expressions) and verbal (tone, rate, volume, inflection, feeling words, and content) cues.

A feeling reflection begins with, "I think you feel," "you sound like," or "you look." Such a reflection helps the speaker get in touch with and take ownership of a particular emotion to accurately represent his or her experience. In reflecting feelings, it is important to be tentative and always allow time for the speaker to correct an inaccurate reflection.

The focus in reflecting feelings is the emotion of the other person. Because our "feeling" vocabularies are limited, we often describe feelings inaccurately, and settle for a mild adjective like "upset" when we really mean "furious." Try to use accurate feeling adjectives to avoid this problem.

Feeling reflections are especially important when a listener believes the speaker feels something he or she is not verbalizing. *Door openers* are commonly used in such nonverbal situations. These are non-coercive invitations that encourage a speaker to talk with a statement that expresses the listener's perception of what the speaker is thinking or feeling. Door openers might include comments like, "You seem troubled," "you sure look excited," "you appear upset about something," or "it looks like things really went well."

To utilize a door opener, a listener first says or reflects what he or she sees in the speaker's behavior, then invites the speaker to talk by stating or implying that the listener is able and willing to take time to listen. Finally, the listener waits in silence to see if the speaker wants to talk and listens reflectively to the speaker's response.

Reflecting meaning involves listening accurately and reflecting both the content and feelings of the speaker in a single response. Words like "because" or "when" can tie the two together in a sentence: "You feel (feeling word) because (content)." This step puts everything together.

ACKNOWLEDGMENT RESPONSES

These short responses help the speaker know the other party is listening. Examples include nodding and verbalizations such as "um-hum," "uh-huh," "oh," "sure," "go on," "you bet," "you did?" "yes," "sounds good," and "right on."

SUMMARIZING

Summarizing involves listening accurately, condensing the main points of a communication into one to three sentences, and reflecting these back to the speaker. The idea is to capture the essence of the speaker's thoughts and feelings about a particular value or perspective. The reflecting process requires that information be heard in manageable segments. Summarizing after each significant part allows listeners to express their perception of the essence of that segment and check the accuracy of their listening (Katz and McNulty).[25]

Summarizing is different than reflecting. Reflecting involves breaking into a speaker's monologue to capture and restate bite-sized pieces of the communication. Summarizing occurs after the speaker has finished a larger segment and is also useful at the end of a conversation to capture its essence and bring the communication to a close. Summarizing includes phrases such as, "To recap" or, "I'd like to make sure I."

Listeners should not summarize at the beginning of a conversation with comments like, "I feel you are really upset about." Such statements tend to anger or frustrate speakers, who feel they are being psychoanalyzed rather than understood. In general, it is better to avoid preambles when constructing reflective responses because they distract from the reflections offered.

A preamble may sometimes be useful at the start of a reflection to help listeners assess the accuracy of their understanding or to express confusion about what a speaker is saying. If you trust that your perceptions of what a speaker is trying to say are accurate and the speaker is receptive, such phrases might begin with, "From your point of view," "as you see it," "in your experience," or "you believe." If you are having trouble clearly perceiving what another person is trying to say or believe that the speaker may not be receptive, such phrases might start, "It seems like," "what I guess I'm hearing is that" or "it appears that you."

A conversation when one or both parties don't listen causes a lack of understanding, respect, consideration, and a desire not to be in that moment. It is fine if you don't want to continue a conversation, but how you act at that point must ease you out efficiently, while creating a positive finish and an empathic and calm ending. In this way, both the speaker and listener can leave a conversation with mutual respect.

CLARIFYING TO DIG DEEPER

Active listening is more than simply hearing what speakers say and reflecting their statements to create mutual understanding. To be truly effective, listeners must determine a speaker's problem or deeper issues through meaningful, discovery questions. According to Tom Freese, president of QBS Research and author of five best-selling sales books, "The questions you ask are more important than the things you could ever say." Not only do such questions show the speaker that you are a terrific listener, but they allow you to dig deeper and put yourself in a position to help solve the speaker's problems or add value in a unique way (Osten).[26]

These questions are another part of the active listening process and can be used both during and after reflections. To *clarify* what you hear from others, use prompts like "Can you help me understand more?" "What did you mean by that?" "Can you walk me through what you were trying to accomplish?" or "Can you give me more details so we can better identify more of the issues and key areas that need to be addressed?" (For the record, "What?" is not a great question.)

This clarification process early in the listening cycle allows the speaker to share more about the topic and expand their initial comments. Ask open versus closed questions using what, when, how, why, and where versus yes or no. These show that you are actively listening (Osten).[27] The process allows speakers to share their feelings and problems and encourages them to "empty their bucket" and go into more detail about a situation, concern, story, or issue. It also helps speakers confirm not only what is on the surface of their mind but their innermost feelings. Author Anthony Robbins echoes this idea: "Successful people ask better questions and as a result, they get better answers" (Robbins).[28] Clarity is key to a deep, full understanding of what is being communicated.

BENEFITS OF REFLECTIVE LISTENING

"Good listeners strive to fully understand what others want to communicate, particularly when a statement lacks clarity" (Doyle).[29]

Reflective listening replaces assumed agreement with verified understanding between speakers and listeners, promotes more balanced conversations, and creates feelings of respect, consideration, and trust. The process results in a warmer, calmer, less hostile, nonjudgmental environment that encourages problem-solving and conflict resolution at work and in social situations with friends and family. The process keeps families together, makes the work environment more open and engaging, and strengthens and lengthens relationships.

Reflective listening provides many benefits to speakers. It helps them more clearly articulate their thoughts; allows them to deal more effectively with emotions and express feelings at a deeper level; and provides a vehicle to help them sort issues, decide on a course of action, and solve their own problems at a comfortable pace (Katz and McNulty). Reflective listening keeps the attention on speakers and allows them to achieve what they want to accomplish in a conversation.

The process is also beneficial for listeners. Reflecting demonstrates to a speaker that the listener is attentive and involved. The frequent reflection restatements also keep both parties engaged in communication and prevent listeners from tuning out of a conversation.

Reflection also allows listeners to check their accuracy and facilitates a clear understanding of what the speaker is trying to say; provides an effective process to deal with issues, problems, and needs raised during a conversation; and is especially well-suited to confirm the specifics of what a listener has agreed to do following a communication. Although both the speaker and listener may believe they agreed on a given course of action, unless the specifics are reflected effectively, the parties may leave the exchange with different expectations of what will be done. Reflective listening is a powerful tool that enhances the quality of all interpersonal communications.

TOTAL LISTENING AND EMPATHY

"People will never forget how you made them feel."
Maya Angelou

Research supports the many benefits of *active listening*. Active listeners show their interest by asking questions, and subtly communicate to the speaker that they're listening through body language and other cues ("Effective"). Adding another component of *empathy* creates an even more powerful listening tool, which I call **total listening**.

Empathy is the ability to sense another person's emotions and attempt to relate to their feelings. President Obama championed empathy as a moral emotion all should cultivate:

> [T]o see the world through the eyes of those who are different from us — the child who's hungry, the steelworker who's been laid off, the family who lost the entire life they built when the storm came…. When you think like this — when you choose to broaden your ambit of concern and empathize with the plight of others, whether they are close friends or distant strangers — it becomes harder not to act, harder not to help.[30]

It is important not to confuse empathy and sympathy. While sympathy only aims to mentally identify a struggling person's emotion, empathy achieves an internal connection with that person (Yugay).[31] *Empaths* have remarkably high sensitivity to the emotions and energy of animals, people, and elements of the environment. They are highly aware of the feelings, tones, nuances, subtexts, and energy currents of all facets of their surroundings.[32]

Although the vast majority of people are not empaths, we can all become more empathic by becoming better listeners. Empathic individuals dive into the very life and issues they are trying to understand, learn how others are feeling, and feel for them.

In his 1933 book, *Down and Out in Paris and London*, George Orwell revealed and unveiled the neglected and marginalized communities in British society. To do so, he walked in the shoes of everyday working people to discover what their lives were really like. This empathic man did not just imagine the lives of the downtrodden; he lived among them and learned everything he could about their lives.

In some ways, active and empathic listening are similar. Each focuses completely on the speaker to get a true, clear understanding of what he or she says. Both recommend facing a speaker during conversation, resisting distractions, and being considerate of the other party's input. Both involve responses that increase shared understanding and trust, and both require giving support and encouragement rather than advice or criticism. Listening empathically, however, entails making an emotional connection with a speaker through identification, compassion, understanding, feeling, and insight; and finding similarities between his or her experiences and your own to give a more heartfelt response (Bhasin).[33]

WHAT IS EMPATHIC LISTENING?

Empathic listening is a structured listening and questioning technique that allows the listener to develop and enhance relationships with a stronger understanding of what is being conveyed, both intellectually and emotionally. Empathic listening is about developing a deep understanding of a speaker beyond the nods, listening posture and sounds of active listening. As such, it takes active listening to a new level ("Empathic"). Hitesh Bhasin, CEO of Marketing91, defines empathic listening as, "Listening with an intent to care with the feeling of compassion and emotional understanding."[34]

Empathic responses show speakers that listeners are personally interested in them and have made them a priority. Empathic listening helps speakers feel better and resolve deep, important issues that are on their mind. Statements like, "You're not alone in experiencing this stress at school," "like you, many others are nervous about starting a new job," or "it's very common to feel anxious because you are speaking at a conference next week" build rapport and create an empathic surrounding by reflecting what the speaker is feeling and experiencing.

Total listening incorporates empathy into the listening process to help advisors become more complete listeners and bring their listening skills to a whole new level. Total listening is a game changer that will differentiate you *immediately and forever* from your competition. Let's examine a few examples. A client is experiencing challenges with both health and family dynamics, and they share some of these concerns and worries with you. First, reflect their comments to elicit more details specific to their situation. "So, it sounds like you're experiencing some health issues and are nervous about how the family is dealing with them." Then, add empathy, "Many people experience these same problems and are in the same boat. I know how you are feeling, so let's talk about how to deal with your concerns and current situation. Tell me more about what's happening."

Empathy is effective in all situations. If a friend is having difficulties at work or a child is having problems at school, first listen attentively and reflect to get clarification. "It sounds like your ideas are being ignored at work" or "you think that your low grade on the project proves the teacher didn't like your work and now you feel stressed at school. Is that right?" Then, add empathy before moving the conversation forward to address or resolve the problem, "This kind of thing happens often. You're not alone here."

DEVELOPING AND DISPLAYING EMPATHY AT WORK

Listen to understand, not to answer. Be authentic. Empathy cannot be forced or faked, which makes it both a powerful leadership skill, and one that is tricky for some people to develop.

Read, research, listen, and learn about others. To avoid judging a particular person or group, dig further and learn more about their particular story or set of beliefs. This could mean taking the time to chat with them or doing some research on the internet. When a conversation involves judgment or opinion, take a breath, pause, and take a moment to think first before responding. Write down objections rather than tuning out a presenter ("Enhancing"). Be open to new ideas and ways of thinking. Look for opportunities to share common ground with the speaker, such as beliefs, ideologies, or experiences.

Many of us routinely judge what others say as we hear them speak. In order to start from a place of open-mindedness and acceptance, make sure you are committed to do all the following *before* entering into a conversation: stay fully present and listen deeply, refrain from judging what the speaker says, interpreting his experience, and offering advice. Avoiding these patterns will enable you to focus more on what the speaker is saying, and less on your own interpretation (Osten).[35]

CHARACTERISTICS OF EMPATHIC LISTENERS

Open Mindedness

As an advisor, an essential first step to building empathy is being self-aware, which means being conscious of your own thoughts and feelings and listening to a speaker's problems or issues without preconceptions or bias (Bhasin).[36]

Listeners should try to enter a conversation with a mind like a blank slate and be willing to be influenced by what they hear. They must avoid anticipating what they think someone is going to say or jumping to conclusions, but instead hear the speaker out entirely and try to understand his or her lines of argument ("Enhancing").

> Listen! All I ask is that you listen. Don't talk or do - just hear me. Advice is cheap and I can do for myself. I am not helpless. Maybe discouraged and faltering, but not helpless. When you do something for me that I can and need to do for myself, you contribute to my fear and inadequacy…. [W]hen you accept … that I feel what I feel, no matter how irrational, then I can stop trying to convince you and get about … understanding what's behind this … feeling. And when that's clear, the answers are obvious, and I don't need advice. Irrational feelings make sense when we understand what's behind them (Kaplowitz).[37]

Suspend Judgment

Suspending judgment requires listeners to try to understand communication from the speaker's viewpoint and seek common ground with the speaker. This doesn't mean listeners must automatically agree with a given statement. Instead, they should put themselves in the speaker's shoes and try to view the arguments presented from that perspective.

One major goal for empathic listening is to identify a speaker's perspective without coloring it with your own. "Seek first to understand, then to be understood" (Covey).[38] This includes refraining from criticizing a speaker, either aloud or to yourself. Listeners should keep arguments supporting their viewpoints to themselves and stay focused on the speaker.

Judgmental listening also occurs when listeners only listen to determine whether a speaker is right or wrong, rather than to understand the speaker's ideas, both emotionally and in terms of content. "This kind of judgmental listening prevents the listener from fully engaging with the speaker on his or her own terms, and therefore limits the scope of the conversation" ("Enhancing").

Maintaining a "no judgment zone" produces stronger, truer, and more meaningful conversations because it lets the listener assess what the speaker says and how it is presented more accurately, which ultimately leads to better understanding of the thoughts, opinions, and feelings of others ("Enhancing").

Tolerance

Tolerance is the willingness to accept others and their beliefs, even if one doesn't necessarily agree with them ("English Club"). Today's world is so filled with political division that people have lost friendships, family, work relationships, and even clients due to conversations surrounding politics. Tolerance is tough in an arena where participants rarely change their mind about a politician or issue, yet we continue to engage others in an argumentative, defensive, often hostile manner to insist that their stance is incorrect.

Antagonistic responses like, "How can you think that?" or "you are absolutely wrong" do not effectively accomplish any of the listening principles.

If you want to keep those family members, friends, or clients, instead of fruitlessly trying to change their opinion, take a new and fresh approach: change your tone, create some reflection, add some empathy, and keep the peace. That way, you'll be able to maintain your relationships and still get invited to holiday dinners. Tolerance allows listeners to get out of their comfort zone and expand their social circle. For example, you might realize that you really enjoy someone's company who you would have avoided if you hadn't consciously *tried* to listen to and understand them ("English Club").

How often do you go to a party or family function and get cornered by some annoying person that you have no desire to speak to, or get stuck on a train beside someone who's driving you nuts? When I'm forced to hear a long-winded tale for the umpteenth time, I don't want to upset my hosts or relatives by being rude. I also don't want to cause a scene on the train by telling some stranger to shut up and being forced to find a new seat. I want to be tolerant of others *and* keep my sanity (Scott).[39]

TIPS TO BE MORE TOLERANT

- Listen carefully without jumping to conclusions. It's easy to blow someone off as soon as they strike up a conversation, although you're nodding politely (Scott). *Really* listen to the speaker. Don't be put off by their appearance or because someone else mentioned they're a little weird. Listen to them, at least for a while. We all want and deserve to be heard.

- Try to understand the other person's point of view. Resist the urge to totally discount what they say because it sounds odd. If you're not sure about their point, ask questions.

- Perhaps the speaker isn't expressing their idea as clearly as they think.

- Agree to disagree. You might not agree with the speaker's opinions. That's fine. We're all different. It doesn't mean that you must become their best friend or switch to their way of thinking, but once you accept that it's okay to "agree to disagree" it will be much easier to have discussions with a variety of people.

Presence

More than just being physically in the same space with a speaker, presence entails being focused closely on the conversation. To be present, it is important to minimize external distractions and refrain from planning responses while another person is talking (Bhasin).[40]

Compassion

The main component of empathic listening is to identify with the speaker's emotional experience, even if a listener hasn't undergone the same situation. For instance, if a coworker says they are having trouble adjusting to an increased workload, a listener may identify by thinking of a time when he or she had more chores at home. Empathic responding is when the listener consistently reflects to the speaker *both* the feeling the speaker is experiencing and the reason for that feeling (as expressed by the speaker).

Being close and caring is the cornerstone of listening in the workplace and one's personal life. Making others feel that their views are important and legitimate creates and maintains strong working and personal relationships (Bhasin).[41]

Wisdom

Someone shares something emotionally important because they trust the judgment and experience of a listener. "Wisdom includes both understanding the speaker's input and examining the circumstances around the problem to better grasp all the factors involved" ("Empathic"). For example, if one colleague shares a conflict with another, a wise listener can acknowledge the speaker's stress while also expressing that the third party might have their own challenges and may not be deliberately trying to be offensive.

Trustworthiness

When another person speaks about emotional matters, it's crucial to keep what they say in confidence. However, if they ask the listener to mediate a conflict with a third party, the listener may discuss details of the conversation if it helps achieve the speaker's goal.

Patience

Even with close colleagues and friends, it can be challenging to disclose emotional experiences. "It may take the speaker some time to find the words for what they want to say and feel comfortable enough to express them" (Bhasin).

Be patient and allow them the time they need to speak freely. Speakers want to feel comfortable enough to express themselves.

Responsiveness

Although empathic listening requires that listeners do not interject their personal views while a speaker has the floor, there is a time to respond. Sometimes, a speaker requests to hear what a listener thinks. In that case, the listener should verify this by asking, "Would you like to hear what I think about this?" or "what kind of feedback would you like from me?"

Negotiating Loss

We are all carriers. We either carry praise, hope, optimism, solutions, gratitude, empathy, understanding, compassion, patience, encouragement, motivation, tolerance, and perseverance **or** we carry fear, criticism, anger, frustration, pessimism, judgment, and complaint. What do you carry? How about your clients, friends, and family? The bigger question is, what do your customers and clients *feel* you are carrying?

People so urgently want to be heard because many are in pain and need to vent, or desperately want to solve a serious problem.

Take, for instance, the many restrictions, issues, and negative effects caused by the COVID pandemic. During the lockdowns and shutdowns, we suffered the loss of connectivity; independence; the freedom to visit malls, movie theatres, sports events, stores, workplaces, and libraries; the ability to attend schools and religious services; and even the means to visit family or travel freely. We lost jobs and family stability and suffered both physical and mental health issues as we buried friends and loved ones. Whether with others or alone, we were prevented from leaving our homes, entertaining visitors, or assisting elderly neighbors.

During the pandemic, people just wanted someone to listen. They didn't need an advisor to downplay their feelings, concerns, or comments. They weren't looking for "an expert" to challenge their opinions or tell them what to think. They simply wanted someone to help them stay afloat during a hard time.

Everyone we know in the workplace and our personal lives is now experiencing or has suffered some traumatic loss. We must enable others to vent, vocalize their pain, and share their thoughts and feelings (empty their bucket) to help them move through the stages of grief, develop coping mechanisms, and work toward acceptance. Empathic listening is key with comments like, "Help me understand more," and "I've felt like that myself."

Providing outlets for those going through loss empowers them; helps them create a plan for their new normal; and aids in overcoming their isolation, loneliness, and fear. Empathic listening allows the bereaved to celebrate the things that are good and build on any positives in their lives. Most important, empathy assures them that they are not alone.

Connectivity

Total listeners are also strong in connectivity by taking the initiative, showing concern, and checking in with others. They stay in touch and remain connected to those around them. They are both active and proactive; and are motivated "not to hide" but to max communication to every client, all friends and family. This separates top advisors forever from their competition and our clients, family and friends will always remember that we were right there by their side, navigating through tough times and helping them get through challenging periods. This is not just for the top clients but for *every* client and *all professional and personal relationships.* It takes time but it's worth it.

That's why we say "thank you" to everyone, compliment others throughout the day, and take the time to let people share. *People like to* talk, and they feel good when they can express themselves.

Don't forget to check in with clients. Do they want you to connect with their kids, attorneys, accountants, or insurance specialists? Would they like you to reach out to other family members or neighbors who may be suffering and need a conversation with you? Be there and available to help them help others.

Always end an empathic conversation with a reassuring close like, "We can make this work or improve what you were worried about" or "yes, it's a tough situation but we will get through it together, now that we understand how you feel."

When I close, I always remind others of the most important thing and say, "We are all in this together and we will come out of this together — stronger, more resilient, and more compassionate." Comments like this bring calm, peace, assurance, confidence, and relief to others. They realize that you have their best interest at heart in both good and challenging times.

CHAPTER 8

OVERCOMING OBJECTIONS AND CHALLENGES

"The most basic of all human needs is to understand and be understood. The best way to understand people is to listen to them."
Ralph Nichols

Wouldn't it be easy if clients and customers didn't raise objections? Advisors could present a solution, product, or strategy and then the client would understand completely, see the benefits, and go with that decision. That would be perfect, but not realistic.

It is human nature to have questions or, more often, object to an advisor's advice, solutions, and strategies. People raise objections for a wide variety of reasons. There is a natural resistance to change, the solution presented may not fully address their needs, they don't see enough value in a product or service, or they are simply too busy or not educated enough on the subject. Regardless of the reason, most advisors do not manage objections well. By being better listeners, advisors can deal with objections more effectively and grow their business.

WHAT THE EXPERTS SAY

To learn how to manage rejection, salespeople must *seek out* rejection: "Ask for what you want directly, assumptively, assertively and repeatedly" (Rusoff). According to Jeb Blount, CEO of Sales Gravy and famed author, "Asking is everything in sales. When you fail to ask, you fail" (Blount).[42]

Advisors and others selling products and services who maintain emotional control in sales scenarios have the highest probability of getting to "yes." If someone says, "I'm too busy," they respond, "That's exactly why I called." If a prospect says, "I want to think about it," they reply, "When I make big decisions, I like to think about them too." This allows things to slow down so advisors can take control of their emotions and formulate the most effective response (Blount).[43]

According to Blount, *pump and pounce* is the most destructive behavior when dealing with objections. When a prospect or client makes an objection, the advisor immediately starts arguing with them about why they're wrong (Blount).[44] Rusoff concurs and suggests that sellers dealing with someone's money patiently allow the client to put everything on the table and isolate the true objection, rather than arguing about the first thing they hear. She adds that if sellers manage a buyer's micro-commitment objections correctly, buying-commitment objections never emerge because the person has already made the commitment to do business (Rusoff).[45]

HOW A "SELF-DISCLOSURE LOOP" HELPS ADVISORS

When advisors encounter hesitancy to turn over a portion or all of a portfolio, a *self-disclosure loop*[46] allows clients to articulate what's really bothering them. Advisors encourage clients to *self-disclose* or share personal information such as their thoughts, dreams, fears, goals, preferences, and experiences. This is an important way to strengthen relationships and build trust ("Self-Disclosure"). Many advisors simply talk too much. They just pitch, pitch, pitch. But when they're talking, they aren't listening. The self-disclosure loop prompts prospects to disclose everything that's bothering them. And when people talk about themselves, they get a dopamine hit to the brain's pleasure center which makes them feel good and want to reveal even more.

ADVISOR'S ROLE WHILE CLIENTS TELL THEIR STORY

Get out of the way. Don't interrupt with your own story. The more clients say, the more they'll divulge their real concerns and issues — and their objections to collaborating with you (Palumbo).[47]

HOW TO ENCOURAGE A CLIENT TO TALK

Begin with broad, open-ended questions about their dreams and what they hope to do in retirement. Such questions don't cause clients to immediately hide behind an emotional wall. If you start with really hard questions about their money, clients may not give you all the information because they feel they're going to be manipulated. The more clients tell their story, the more they'll like you; and the more they like you, the more likely they'll begin or continue to do business with you. This is also a trust issue. The more completely you allow clients to voice their concerns and demonstrate your ability to handle their objections, the better likelihood of success for a positive and meaningful relationship.

IMPORTANCE OF EMPATHY IN THE SALES SCENARIO

As discussed in the previous chapter, empathy is the meta skill of today's modern society. In the professional services industry, advisors are asking another human being to trust them with their future. Empathy allows advisors to step into a prospect's shoes and see things from their point of view instead of trying to talk someone out of feeling the way they do. Advisors must minimize client fears while maximizing the value of collaborating with them to gently help clients make decisions (Rusoff).[48]

The key to empathy is literally closing one's mouth and actively listening to understand the client. Advisors with little empathy try to get as much as they can out of a conversation with the least amount of emotional investment and time. Those high on the empathy scale intentionally ask a client to move to the next step. These advisors frequently have difficulty being assertive and asking for what they want because they feel they're being too pushy.

THE PROCESS TO OVERCOME OBJECTIONS

Client objections are often a *request for more clarification*. It's important to understand a customer's underlying concerns. You want your client to succeed, and you deserve to be paid because your advice has value. The following is a step-by-step approach to handle and overcome objections more effectively.

1. *Listen to the objection and hear what the person says* without responding, solving the problem, or answering.

2. *Reflect back what you heard* to ensure that you heard correctly. "It sounds (seems) like you feel that."

3. *Clarify what you heard* to identify the true objections and deep-rooted concerns or issues. "Help me understand more (tell me more) about that," or "help me understand how that works (what that means)."

4. Listen again to the speaker clarify an objection or issue.

5. *Use your empathy and understanding.* "I totally understand. Many others feel the same way. You're not alone. I hear that often."

6. *Apologize.* "I'm sorry you feel like this (I feel bad that you're going through this). Let's try to deal with this."

7. *Respond.* Assess the client's willingness to find solutions, discover where you can assist or reach out on their behalf, and research the issue. "I find one way

to manage that is," or "here are a few things that have worked for (others) me in that situation."

8. *Clarify again.* Check to see if your solutions, strategies, and choices are acceptable to the client.

9. *Close.* Close that objection. Whether or not a sale is made or a deal accomplished, *always* thank the client for their time and for voicing their concerns.

Effective Responses to Specific Objections

***Objection:* "It's not the right time" or "I'm not interested."** These may be the most common objections advisors hear. These are ways of saying, "I don't want to buy now." The client might be uneasy about an internal or external issue such as family, business difficulties, the economy or the market. They are uncertain.

Don't say: "What are you waiting for? When will be the right time? Will it ever come?"

Instead: Try drawing the client out. What are their concerns? Many people focus on the negatives and overlook the positives. Put these on the table and explain how they tie into your recommendations. Advisors are meant to advise. Suggest a positive course of action when a client is hesitant to act on their own.

***Objection:* "Let me think about it."** That's another way of saying, "I don't want to buy now." The prospect is seeking to push the decision off. There could be many reasons.

Don't say: "That's understandable. I'm going to leave the room for a moment." (You return.) "Okay, you've had a chance to think about it. Glad we got that out of the way." This is not only very "old school" but also notoriously ineffective. The public has become much less tolerant of "hard sell tactics" and this is the very reason auto, timeshare and insurance sales representatives often have poor reputations with customers.

Instead: "Based on your situation, I think this is the right course of action for you (briefly review reasons). It sounds like I'm missing something. Tell me about it."

Objection: "I need to speak with my spouse." Sometimes, the dynamic of any big decision requires the input and consent of multiple parties. The prospect might be stalling but making any type of investment is often a joint decision. That's a potential impediment to moving forward. You may feel the prospect may be unable to explain your proposal the way you presented it.

Don't say: "No problem. (Pick up the phone, put on speaker.) We'll call your spouse now. What's the number?"

Instead: "That makes good sense. I'd like to have the opportunity to meet with both of you, so I can understand your situation and present my proposal personally. Can you both come back tomorrow, or can we meet at your place?"

Objection: **"I already have an advisor."** The client sees the advisor's role as standardized. They have one mechanic, one barber, and one accountant. They don't see the need for more.

Don't say: "But they aren't as good as me. Ditch them. You are moving into the big leagues now."

Instead: "Successful people often have multiple advisory relationships. You're obviously successful. How many do you have?" Another approach is, "How many doctors do you have?"

Objection: **"I'm waiting until after the election, tax season or the holidays."** Some people are hesitant to act in times of uncertainty or use the calendar as an excuse to procrastinate.

Don't say: "Don't tell me you're afraid to make decisions."

Instead: "Think beyond these events. Look toward trends which are likely to continue. Significant dates will always occur, but in order to achieve your goals and help you now and in the future, it makes sense for us to move forward with this proposal. Tell me your thoughts and how I can help you get started."

Objection: **"Call me in six months."** The client might be saying, "I don't want to focus on this at the present time."

Don't say: "I need your business now. I have numbers to hit." This is a negative, unprofessional, high-pressure approach.

Instead: "Here's why I think we should be in position now. This proposal makes sense for both your short-term needs and your long-term goals. I feel comfortable that this proposal meets your objectives, and we should move forward."

***Objection:* "You're new to this. You don't have a lot of experience in the industry."** The client is concerned that you may lack expertise and is worried that you will either be practicing on them or will not be able to provide the quality or desired skill set to meet their needs. Take for example, the investment industry.

Don't say: "You are a new investor. We'll learn together. You'll just be the one that puts up the money. How about that?"

Instead: "You are investing with a successful firm that has been in operation for _______ years. I'm part of a team with resources including: ___________. We have (number) clients, and (number) assets under management. Our firm has award-winning research (name a few awards). My job is to provide you with all the resources of my firm to help achieve your goals.

Objection: **"I'm waiting for the economy to be better."** The prospect is hoping there will be a gradual improvement to make them feel more confident to act.

Don't say: "You might be waiting for quite a long time. How old are you?"

Instead: "You're right. The economy does move in cycles and the length of cycles varies. Presently, we are in this environment. What's your money earning now? How long do you think you'll need to wait before you see a change you like? Your money should be working for you in the meantime. Here's the thinking behind my proposal. Let's talk again about what you are trying to accomplish in the long-term, not just in the current economy. What is important to you and how do you want to improve on what you are currently doing?"

Objection: **"You are too expensive."** People incorrectly compare cheap online trading prices with the many additional services provided by an advisor. They don't realize that advice has value.

Don't say: "Compared to what? Investing on your own? Obviously, that isn't working; otherwise, we wouldn't be talking."

Instead: "We provide comprehensive, consultative wealth management. The purchase of actual investments is only a portion of the process. It's important to know where you want to go, and also to have a realistic plan to get there. Working together with our resources, research, and proactive communication as a team and then advising you is how we add value. We apply the most cost-effective and cost- efficient approach. Fees are only an issue absent value added."

OBJECTIONS IN PERSONAL RELATIONSHIPS

What about objections that are not work-related? Those in personal relationships can be handled the same way. Take, for example, our children. They voice a variety of complaints on a daily basis, "I don't want that for dinner," "I don't like school," I want to quit band," "I'm done playing that sport," or "I'm tired and I don't want to go to that family function."

Fortunately, all objections are fundamentally the same. Listen to the comment, clarify the details, probe to discover if the statement is masking a more meaningful, underlying issue, add an empathic response and then overcome the objection with one of the "starters" above. "It sounds like you _________, and I get your frustration (anger, or resentment). It's not the first time someone has felt this way. In fact, I've felt that way myself, but I have found it may benefit you to _________" or "it's my responsibility to help you see that _________."

THE TWO WORLDS OF GENDER LISTENING

Objections can also arise simply due to listening differences between the genders. My wife often reminds me that men and women use different listening strategies. From my personal point of view, it seems that men want to solve (or at least offer a resolution) for every problem or objection, while women simply want to be heard rather than being given a solution. John Gray, author of *Men Are from Mars, Women Are from Venus*, agrees. According to Gray, "Men are motivated when they feel needed while women are motivated when they feel cherished.… Men need to remember that women talk about problems to get close and not necessarily to get solutions."

Frequently, men want to solve a problem right now. Rather than listening, they want to tell a speaker what they should be doing and how to do it, and often interrupt. In a familiar scenario, two couples go out for dinner. One of the wives starts to tell a story to the group but her husband repeatedly interrupts her with his own commentary. She glares at him and says, "Since you want to tell the story, why don't you just go ahead and tell it!" Men are more likely than women to cut off other speakers and take over or dominate conversations. Not always, but frequently, men are louder, and are sometimes more boisterous or obnoxious.

Women are better at reflecting, nurturing, and understanding. They seem more patient and converse with more compassion than men, and more easily involve themselves with emotional discussions. While men want to solve a problem, women want to discuss it.

A survey polled one hundred mental health professionals and found that communication problems were cited as the most common factor that led to divorce (65%), followed by a couple's inability to resolve conflict (43%) (Bilow).[49]

The survey also found that men and women have different communication complaints. Men cite nagging and complaining as the top communication problem in their marriage (70%) while women's top complaint (83%) was that their spouse didn't validate their opinions or feelings enough (Billow).[50]

> When a man can listen to a woman's feelings without getting angry and frustrated, he gives her a wonderful gift. He makes it safe for her to express herself. The more she is able to express herself, the more she feels heard and understood and the more she is able to give a man the loving trust, acceptance, appreciation, admiration, approval, and encouragement that he needs (Gray).[51]

A question to ponder: What would your significant other say if I asked them if you were a great listener?"

In today's world of multi-gender sensitivity, understanding and respecting how an individual wishes to be addressed and effectively communicating and responding to objections in an appropriate fashion will require even stronger listening and clarification skills.

CHAPTER 9

BENEFITS OF GOOD LISTENING IN THE WORKPLACE

*"Listening to others' viewpoints may reveal the
one thing needed to complete your goals."*
D. Ridgley

You might wonder why advisors need communication skills in the workplace. The stereotype of fiscal experts is that they're much better with numbers than with words. While this may be valid for some entry-level positions, it simply isn't true for upper management. In fact, good listening is especially critical in accounting, as advisors deal with financial records and other elements that could affect a client's livelihood and financial future ("The Benefits").

Evidence shows that listening is a highly valued skill sought by all employers ("Why Is Listening"). Listening in a work context is the process a listener uses to better understand the needs, demands, and preferences of stakeholders through direct interaction (Doyle). Stakeholders include everyone in the workplace from your boss, client, coworker, subordinate, board member, or interviewer to a job candidate.

Good listeners are more likely to understand tasks and projects, build stronger relationships with coworkers, and be able to solve problems and resolve conflicts ("Effective"). How well you listen may be the single biggest factor in the success of your career and the quality of all your relationships.

THE RESEARCH

A great deal of research highlights the importance of good listening for those in revenue-generating roles. According to HubSpot's most recent customer satisfaction (CSAT) data, 69% of buyer respondents said the top thing required for a positive experience is that "the sales representative listens to my needs" ("The Ultimate")[52]. Further, according to thousands of NPS surveys from both clients and employees, the number one driver of buyer loyalty is that they feel "someone takes the time *to listen* to my needs and wants" ("What is NPS?").[53]

Many people think that good listening entails only not talking when others are speaking, showing interest through facial expressions and verbalizations, and being able to repeat verbatim what others have said. According to a study by Folkman and Zengler, these behaviors alone fall far short of good listening skills. They used responses from almost 4,000 participants in a program to help managers become better coaches, then analyzed the characteristics listed for the top 5% of those rated as outstanding listeners by their peers. The results fall into four main areas.

- *Good listening is more than being silent while another talks.*

The best listeners periodically ask questions that gently challenge old assumptions in a constructive way to promote discovery and insight. This tells the speaker that the listener has not only heard what is said but understands it well enough to want additional information. Good listening is consistently seen as an active, two-way dialogue, rather than a one-way "speaker versus hearer" interaction.

- *Good listeners build the other person's self-esteem.*

The best listeners make conversations positive for others. Rather than being passive or critical, they make speakers feel supported, convey confidence in them, and create a safe environment in which issues and differences can be openly discussed.

- *Good listening is cooperative conversation.*

Feedback flows smoothly in both directions with neither party becoming defensive about comments made by the other. Poor listeners are viewed as competitive, listening only to identify and critically point out errors in reasoning or using their silence as a chance to prepare their next response. Even when good listeners challenge assumptions or disagree, the speaker feels the listener is trying to help rather than attempting to win an argument.

- *Good listeners make positive suggestions.*

Good listening invariably includes some feedback that opens up alternatives to consider, provided in a way others will accept. The skill with which suggestions are made is critical, rather than the suggestions themselves. In addition, others are more likely to accept ideas from people they already believe are good listeners. Someone who is silent for a whole conversation and then jumps in with a suggestion may not be viewed as credible, and someone who seems combative or critical and then tries to give advice may not be seen as trustworthy.

Rather than being a sponge that simply collects what the speaker says, these findings show that good listeners are like trampolines: a safe place from which to bounce ideas. Instead of solely absorbing the speaker's ideas and energy, good listeners amplify, energize, and clarify his or her thinking. This active support makes speakers feel better and gain energy and height, just like someone jumping on a trampoline (Folkman and Zenger).[54]

OVERVIEW

Advisors who listen effectively are more productive because they hear things accurately the first time and aren't forced to make corrections or entirely redo presentations because they originally missed a critical point. Poor listening wastes time, money, and effort; and often causes the loss of customers or employees. I have found that advisors who are good listeners may have a better opportunity to get consistent referrals and new business because they listen efficiently.

In any business setting, being able to listen effectively can go a long way toward understanding client needs, addressing issues or concerns, and providing the best service. Total listening gives both customers and coworkers feelings of ease, comfort, and trust. Harmony replaces workplace discord, disagreement, and frustration. When you listen to others, conversation becomes better, stronger, and more enjoyable. There is more give and take, deeper understanding, less stress, and less confusion. All parties are equally informed and understand one another (Schwantes).[56]

Listening is more than having the patience not to interrupt (Cruse). It is also asking the right questions, engaging with the answers, and dismantling bad habits before attempting to embrace new ones. Advisors are natural problem-solvers. This means that if we are not careful, we can be too quick to rush in with a solution and may miss something important. Sometimes it's better to stand back and take some time to listen.

The total listening process makes clients feel you are working for their benefit, not your own. Clients feel empowered to express what they want you to do for them, how well you are performing to date, and what actions they would like to see increase or decrease in the future. When you listen this way, you will have better conversations and more meaningful dialogue with both colleagues and clients, develop deeper respect for your customers, and become a stronger communicator.

Communication skills make you a more effective workplace leader, build resilience, and help maintain balance in your business relationships. Success *depends* upon your ability to communicate. To be recognized as a confident and efficient communicator, you must first be a good listener (Cruse).[57]

One way to improve listening skills is to minimize comments and use more questions in your conversations. Learning to listen helps you understand and empathize with others and that, in turn, improves your insight and intuition (Plante).[58] People are usually hungry to be heard because they have something weighing on their mind that is creating angst, stress, and anxiety. That person is trying to share or vent to relieve their burden. When you don't listen, they become disappointed, frustrated, and angry. Their tension and frustration build and can lead to poor decision-making.

Our brain works in two different ways regarding decisions. Quick decisions are not contemplated. They are short, intuitive, impulsive, and reactive. Rational, thought-out decisions take more time and are based on hearing advice, listening to reason, and using logic. When our brains are filled with pressure, anxiety, stress, and worries, we tend to make snap judgments. We advisors are stepping in our own way and making it difficult for our clients to make informed, rational decisions. We could make things much easier by simply listening a little better (Palumbo).[59]

Total listening helps us focus on understanding others and improves our relationships by promoting trust, reducing conflict, and increasing our ability to motivate and inspire those with whom we're communicating. Listening to people's stories, along with sharing our own, can prompt us to put ourselves into their world, which cultivates connection and empathy (Osten).[60]

LISTENING IMPROVES CLIENT RELATIONSHIPS

- *Listening improves the level of trust.*

"Authentic listening generates respect and trust between talker and listener" (Schwantes).[61] Trust increases when clients know their advisor listens intently to their issues and works to resolve them. They appreciate it when advisors treat them as partners, and they do not have to repeat themselves.

- *Listening enhances the advisor's credibility.*

Credibility is key in effective client relationships. Customers want to collaborate with advisors who give them advice based on the information they have provided. This builds credibility and significantly improves the advisor-client relationship ("The Benefits").[62]

- *Listening increases customer service levels.*

Client relationships improve when customer service is effective. Good listening skills minimize the chance of mistakes or misinterpretations and are an integral tool in developing superior customer service ("How Listening Can Help").[63]

- *Listening increases customer loyalty.*

Effective listening leads clients to your doorstep. Customers who are pleased with your work become loyal and do not want to use anyone else for their transactions or services.

LISTENING IMPROVES WORKPLACE FUNCTIONALITY

- *Listening increases productivity.*

Problems are solved faster if people are encouraged to explain issues and given the freedom to work though solutions aloud before being told what to do.

- *Listening helps both sides stay calm when dealing with a crisis or discussing a sensitive issue.*

Rather than solely planning their rebuttal or tuning out during disagreements, effective listening allows all parties to focus on the issues at hand and arrive at rational solutions.

- *Listening boosts confidence.*

Great listeners have better self-esteem and a more positive self-image because effective listening allows them to establish positive relationships with their colleagues (Schwantes).[64]

- *Listening reduces mistakes.*

Good listening leads to more accuracy in retaining information. A clearer memory of important facts minimizes the risk of miscommunication or errors.

EXAMPLES OF EFFECTIVE WORKPLACE LISTENING

- A job candidate reflects her understanding of an unclear question during an interview and asks for more details.
- An interviewer notes a candidate doesn't look her in the eye when asserting a key skill and asks a follow-up question to learn more about how he has applied it in a past job.
- A customer service worker reflects a complaint back to a patron to reassure the customer that he has been heard.

- A meeting facilitator compliments a shy team member, then asks him to share his views about a proposal.
- After a manager summarizes team comments during a staff meeting, she asks if she has heard them correctly.
- An employee restates all the specific areas which his supervisor has asked him to improve at the end of a performance review.
- At a client meeting, the advisor asks an open-ended question to encourage the customer to fully express any concerns.
- An employee carefully listens at a training session and asks insightful questions about the material.

REVIEW OF THE COMMUNICATION CYCLE

The total listening process in workplace communications and negotiations allows you to accurately identify a speaker's concerns, needs, and issues and move their problem toward resolution. You must consciously choose to disregard all distractions and make that speaker your focus, putting everything else aside. This includes putting away your cell phone, turning off your computer, and maintaining eye contact; as well as carefully identifying the speaker's cues. Do they appear nervous, angry, or sad? Are they exhibiting a posture of ease or tension?

Active listening includes the skill of asking good questions. Thoughtful, open-ended queries give the speaker a chance to clarify, open up, and engage in a meaningful dialogue. When used throughout the listening process, they show that you are engaged. "Yeah, I hear you. Yes, that makes sense. Really? What else?"

Avoid hijacking the conversation and turning it toward yourself. Instead, *reflect* as you listen and follow the sequence of the events the speaker explains, "So, this happened to you. Does that sound right?" This shows the speaker you are actually listening to them, care about what they are saying, and value what is important to them, rather than what is important to you. Reflecting reduces barriers to shared understanding such as ignoring the speaker or offering immediate advice and allows your brain to focus on hearing details correctly. This minimizes misinterpreting what you hear versus what others actually say and feel.

It is important to reflect not only the content but also the speaker's feelings. Asking questions like, "What's it like to be experiencing that situation?" or "What's that like for you?" tells the speaker you want to know the emotional burdens they carry, and helps you identify more clearly what they are experiencing. *Reflection* allows the speaker to empty their bucket, vent, and more easily express their emotions.

Empathic statements indicate that you understand what the speaker is experiencing, "If I were going through that, I might feel the same way." "It makes sense that you feel like that." This does not mean you endorse or agree with their feelings. Instead, you are saying that you recognize what they are feeling. "In the situation you described, I could see myself getting sad, angry or frustrated." *Empathy* connects to reflection as you continue the journey to successful listening.

You might want to give advice at this point and tell the speaker what you feel they should or must do, but this is not yet warranted. Before you get to that point, the speaker must be allowed to suggest changes or solutions for him or herself.

When it is appropriate to respond, your statements should be a sharing of your experience and how you have acted in situations similar to those presented by the speaker versus flaunting, preaching, or telling them what they need to do. When a client asks you to listen and you start to give them advice, you have not done what they asked. When they ask that you listen and, instead, you tell them why they shouldn't feel a certain way, you are trampling on their feelings. When you feel compelled to solve a client's problem rather than listening to them, you have failed them ("Warmup").[65]

CHAPTER 10

LISTENING AND LEADERSHIP

"Of all the skills of leadership, listening is the most valuable – and one of the least understood. Most captains of industry listen only sometimes, and they remain ordinary leaders. But a few, the great ones, never stop listening. That's how they get word before anyone else of unseen problems and opportunities."
Peter Nulty

LISTENING AS A LEADERSHIP SKILL

Many of us spend great amounts of time and energy to develop skills like time management and public speaking to be successful workplace leaders. But what about taking time to develop the skill of listening?

Although it isn't listed in the job description, effective listening is a vital leadership responsibility (Llopis).[66] Companies, sports teams, performing arts entities, and local, state, or Federal governmental bodies all require strong leadership — and successful leaders possess top listening skills. Leaders who are empathic, patient, and knowledgeable listeners get the clients and improve their bottom-line *because* they listen. By listening to others' concerns and ideas, they can dramatically improve and remove obstacles to optimal business performance.

"Those who listen to their employees are in a much better position to lead their organizations to greater levels of success" (Arcieri).[67] Leaders accomplish most when every team member feels that their voice, concerns, and actions matter. Asking employees questions and listening to what they say makes them feel important and encourages them to view you as a caring leader. If they feel that you care, they will be more productive and increase their contributions to the organization (Acieri).[68]

Leadership success depends on your ability to communicate effectively. Reflective listening, skillful questioning, and the ability to flex communication styles are key to establishing rapport, creating relationships, and getting things done with and through others. Active and focused listening is also the gateway to better decision making, strategy, and bottom-line results, making it critical for leaders to sharpen these skills.

Sometimes, however, leaders are unaware of their listening shortcomings. When a leadership coach received a low rating for listening on a performance assessment, his shocked response was, "Listening is all I do!" He then described how his virtual team called in daily to give him information so he could make decisions and report to the senior team. What he learned from this feedback was that he was not actively listening by acknowledging or communicating back what he had heard. Therefore, he increased his verbal responses and used more prompts to encourage his team to say more. The man gained new insights, and his decision- making became more effective (Seaton).

In another case, an executive fell prey to the common misperception that it is "leaderly" to be dominant and immediately decisive. When interviewed, she admitted that she "tolerated" listening to others but already knew that her mind was made up. In theory, she understood the value of seeking opinions and collaborating, but said she found it physically painful to listen when she had already decided on a course of action. She also defaulted to her style of quick-paced decision-making because she saw this as a "positive leadership attribute." She failed to realize that these actions caused her team to become disengaged. Once she chose to be more purposeful in her listening and learned mindfulness techniques to keep herself "curious" during conversations with others, she was able to value her team more and actually enjoy their individual contributions (Seaton).[69]

TIPS TO IMPROVE LEADERSHIP LISTENING SKILLS

- Engage your employees, treat them as valuable assets who bring unique capabilities and aptitudes to their job functions, and encourage them to share their opinions on all aspects of the workplace. There is too much going on in today's business environment for a leader to know everything. Ensure that when others provide ideas, you truly consider what they are saying and are not thinking about how you are going to respond.

- You can't listen until you are anchored into a conversation. Put away your phone or any distractions. If, for some reason, that isn't possible because of other priorities, be honest and remind yourself to return to the conversation when you can.

- Make eye contact during all communications. Take note of what is said and of how it is said. Don't judge or make harsh criticism when others express different ways of approaching or solving problems.

- Compassionate leaders don't interrupt the flow of conversation. They earn respect from their colleagues by being patient listeners. The best leaders make themselves approachable and show empathy when their employees need attention.

- While it is not possible to implement every idea, evaluating or discussing all suggestions in more detail rather than disregarding them is a great sign you've listened.

- Before you enter a conversation, ask yourself if you would really rather say to the other person, "I'm going to pretend to listen, but I'm actually going to sell you on my own idea." If you answer "yes," you are not ready to listen. If you answer "no," hold yourself accountable to be present and learn as much as you can. It is perfectly okay to say, "Thank you for giving me your perspective but I see things differently and this is how I want us to proceed."

- Sometimes a team member can ramble when given the opportunity. Set a listening period up front, finding language that suits your style. You might say, "I know you have some ideas about this project. If we spent ten minutes on this now, will that give us a good start?"

- Review your conversations at the end of the day and do a listening audit. How many times were you really listening as compared to checking off the box, mentally preparing your next comment, listening impatiently, or over-talking? Seek out a trusted colleague or coach to discuss this.

- Your team wants to be heard. A verbal summary is one way to acknowledge and appreciate the intent of others. Be true to your style and find ways to summarize others' points of view in a way that doesn't sound condescending. A summary is also a useful tool for respectfully ending conversations versus just turning away (Seaton).[70] Consider saying something like, "I can see the decision has an impact on your work. Thank you for giving me your perspective."

- Before conversations, ask the others involved how they want you to listen or what they want from the communication. Does your team want you to listen to seek understanding? Do they want an opportunity to vent? Do they want assistance in problem- solving? Leaders need different skills for each of these listening opportunities. Give your team and colleagues permission to request how they want you to listen. If they don't, be sure to ask.

Everyone has something to say, a story to tell, and words from which we can learn. "I encourage you to listen — really listen — to those around you, whether the speaker is someone you know well or a new personal or professional acquaintance" (Osten).[71] You never know where someone else's words may lead you.

Listening is not easy and learning to do it well deserves a valued place in leadership development. Listening actively and appropriately is at the foundation of respect and leadership success. Today is a great day to assess your own listening skills and start working on ways for improvement.

CHAPTER 11

HOW VALUABLE ARE YOU TO CLIENTS AND PROFESSIONALS?

"You learn more by listening than by talking."
Alyssa McCumber

THE GOLDEN TICKET

When should the advisor talk? When is the right time to share your knowledge, advice, help, guidance, suggestions, and opinions? Finding the right time is the key, the *golden ticket.*

The following question will change your life forever: **"What is most important to you with regard to a relationship with an (advisor, insurance agent, attorney,**

accountant, coach, or teacher)?" It is useful in both professional and personal settings and allows the speaker to be heard while the advisor listens and reflects.

This one question that has helped me the most to win business over my competitors during my career. It employs a process and technique focusing on active listening, opening deeper dialogue, and shifting advisor responses to later in the conversation. This creates meaningful time for the prospect or client to truly empty their bucket and share their concerns, what is profoundly important to them, what specifically they are trying to achieve, and how they want to achieve it.

Notice that this question is not worded to elicit specific comments about you personally or your firm. The words *"to you"* place the focus on the client, and *"a relationship"* does not indicate either their present relationship or a new one with you. This keeps the question objective and the speaker does not become defensive about a prior or current advisor.

Instead, it asks the speaker to focus on his or her important goals and identify what they seek from a relationship with an advisor. This creates an open-ended dialogue to help individuals think beyond today and describe how they envision an advisor will help them meet their present and future goals.

The question begins the reflective listening process. The speaker may reply, "Trust," "communication," or "I want to know that someone hears and listens to me." Immediately *write down* their response. This shows you are taking them seriously.

Then, *reflect and clarify*. "So, when you say communication, share with me what it looks like for you. Help me understand how you see communication that works for you." A speaker's first answer may be superficial but there is often a deeper and more pressing issue that is bothering them, or something significant they want to accomplish or seek help with.

Ask what else is important to them. When they mention additional goals or concerns, write them down and let the customer discuss each one with you and share what they are missing and what they are looking for. Ask open versus closed questions eliciting what, when, how, why, and where versus "yes or no" answers. Some examples might be, "What are some ways?" "How did you accomplish that?" "What are the steps?" or "Where did your concerns come from?"

Let the speaker empty their bucket of what they like, what they don't, what they want, and what they feel will be helpful to them. You have now created the cornerstone and foundation of a relationship — what is important to *them* rather than *you*.

Use two to three of the answers provided by the speaker as the theme at the next meeting or session when you present your ideas, solutions, and strategies. The client will be amazed and impressed that you listened and remembered what they shared with you; and realize, *Wow! The advisor really listened to me, heard me, and understood what's most important to me. They truly know what I am trying to accomplish and are focused on me, rather than themselves.*

THE OPEN-DOOR MOMENT

Let's say you stop on a street to help a stranger change a tire. Afterwards, they say, "Thank you," or "thank you so much! You don't realize what you've done to help me." When you resolve an issue for a client, assist a person, or help that stranger and receive a "thank you" is the ideal **open-door moment** *to solicit referrals or introductions.*

If you immediately ask that stranger, "Can I ask for your help for one second?" nine times out of ten, they'll reply, "Of course, yes, tell me how I can help you" or "what can I do to help you?" At such an *open-door moment,* you have an almost 100% chance to obtain a referral. All you have to do is listen for the opportunity.

If that's true, why do many professionals find it so difficult to seek referrals and prefer that they come unsolicited? Typically, the request makes them afraid or uncomfortable. They lack confidence that a customer will offer a referral or feel that the request will put a client in an uncomfortable situation that will hurt their relationship.

By far, however, the biggest reason that clients and customers don't give referrals is because professionals don't ask for them!

HOW TO EFFECTIVELY ASK FOR REFERRALS

Getting referrals begins with recognizing the opportunity. Be an attentive listener when a client shares their satisfaction and pleasure with your service or advice. Let them talk, and if they give you or your firm a compliment, be appreciative and follow up with these five steps to maximize referrals.

1. Thank the speaker back when you get a thank you, "No, thank *you*. We love doing this."

2. Ask for help, "Oh, by the way, can I ask you for help?"

3. If the client responds that they may not get the same level of service and attention if they recommend you, or that you might get too big for them,

immediately address these concerns, "We've added some additional technology and services that we have identified this year, so we have the capacity to take on five additional households that look just like yours." (Most of the time clients will give you a name on the spot. If not, follow up within a few days to see if they were able to think of anyone.)

4. If you get a referral, identify the client's background. Do you know them personally, recreationally, via philanthropy, or through business?

5. Now ask for their advice. Why? Because the experts agree that if you seek and receive guidance, the advising party is strongly committed to seeing their recommendations succeed. "Just one more quick thing. If you were me, how would you go about gaining that introduction?"

SURVEY CLIENTS TO GET EFFECTIVE FEEDBACK

Although it takes time, surveys raise the client experience and benefit your relationship by obtaining effective feedback. Professional service industries historically have sent out surveys after services are rendered. Since customer retention is vital in the competitive market of today, surveys can now be conducted through video conferencing, telephone or in person. Surveys should be client-focused and designed to determine what your firm is doing well, and what experiences your customers are missing or not getting.

The following are some sample questions for clients.

- "What are three things we do well? Tell me more."
- "Rate your overall experience on a scale of 1-10 with 10 being the greatest possible experience." Follow up with, "Why do you feel that way?"
- "Rate us in the areas of courtesy and responsiveness." As a follow-up, ask, "If you could change one thing we do, what would that be?"
- "When you think of the services we provide, what words come to mind?" You can also give the client a brochure with the comment, "Instead of asking what we do, let us have our best customers tell you what we do and how we do it."

KEYS FOR SUCCESS AT THE FOLLOW-UP MEETING

If advisors use high-level listening skills to ask open-ended questions in an appropriate way at their follow-up meeting, it will lead to stronger, happier client relationships. The more clients feel we are listening, the more they feel we are on their side and aligned with them.

Likeability is just as important as industry knowledge. Don't forget those open-door moments that appear during ongoing conversations with your current and new customers. You will be amazed that you still don't know many things, even about clients you have been servicing for years.

For example, think about what you know regarding a customer's family and history. Clients love to talk about family. Touch on the little things. Ask questions like, "What is your favorite way to spend time with your family and why?" or "What makes for a great family vacation? Tell me more. Can you expand on that?" It is vital for advisors to ask questions and even more important to listen to our clients. We must be able to act, react and respond quickly; monitor in real time; and make comprehensive, rather than piecemeal, moves.

Charitable intentions are also important to many of your relationships, as most affluent clients are active in this area. At your next client meeting, in addition to discussing their survey responses, you might open a conversation on this issue by saying, "As you know, we like to participate in charities and organizations that are most important to our clients. What community groups and charities do you support that you feel we should be more involved with?"

Even an accountant or tax CPA who meets with a client only once or twice a year can learn a great deal from asking lifestyle questions. Some examples might be, "What are your hobbies and interests? What is the best trip you have ever taken? Why? Tell me about it. What are you passionate about? What would like to spend more time doing?"

If you are a family counselor or estate planning attorney, perhaps life events can be a focus of the conversation and your questions. For example, "What plans have you made in the event you are disabled? What is on the horizon for your children? (weddings, anniversaries, college, babies, homes). Tell me about any major event that you anticipate over the next twelve months or the next few years. What have you always wanted to do that you have not been able to do thus far?"

We want our clients to think of their advisor as a key part of their *inner circle*. To reach that pinnacle of trust requires that advisors practice the highest level of listening. That inner circle advisor for the client's family or company is someone they can contact when they are feeling good but also someone who is always watching out for their best interests. Once an advisor is part of the inner circle, a client **never** wonders, *Other than my money, do they have a clue of what I am* *all about? Am I really important to them?* or *are they the right people to get me to the next phase in life?* and the relationship will last and even strengthen over time.

CHAPTER 12

QUESTIONS AND RESPONSES FOR ADVISORS

"Great leaders are great listeners who know their best asset is the people they work with. Lead by listening – to be a good leader you have to be a great listener."
Richard Branson

It is important that advisors speak in a way that makes others love to listen to them but even *more* vital for them to listen in a way that makes others love speaking with them ("Richard Branson Biography").[72] You must practice building good listening habits while avoiding bad ones. If you develop the habit of listening and the skills to listen effectively, others will like you better and will listen to you more. As Jim Collins discusses in *Good to*

Great, this *likeability* factor is critical to differentiating great leaders from good ones.

When speaking with business clients or customers, make sure they are heard. Encourage them to tell a personal story. Let them empty their bucket. Reflect their voice and make them your total focus. In any advising relationship, if clients don't feel they are being heard or think you are not hearing them clearly, it's game over no matter what you do, how good you are, or how well you serve them.

Good listening skills are vital in the workplace. Potential employers also watch for applicants to demonstrate listening skills during job interviews. In interviews, let the interviewer complete each question or statement before speaking. Do not interrupt and be sure that your reply answers the question. It's perfectly acceptable to take a few moments to frame a precise response. This shows you have fully absorbed the speaker's words and are considerate enough to formulate the best answer.

Asking the right questions is critical to open dialogues, discussions, and conversations. Many of the sample questions that follow ask for three responses. This type of "trilogy" questioning forces the responder to think on a deeper level and provides clearer, more detailed, information to the advisor.

QUESTIONS TO OPEN BUSINESS DISCUSSIONS

- *Set an agenda.* "What three things do you want to accomplish today during this conversation (meeting, call)?"
- *Seek doorways of opportunity.* "What three things do you wish were different in your current advisor relationship?"
- *Use outcomes versus things to determine client values.* "What three outcomes do you hope to achieve through my relationship with you?"
- *Identify passions/purposes.* "What three things do you wish you could spend time doing now?"
- *Discover dreams and goals.* "What three activities do you want to engage in when you (sell your home or business, retire)?"
- *Probe priorities.* "What are the three most important things you would like to do for your family to ensure their security in the future?"
- *Create a safe place to discuss fears, uncertainties, and doubts.* "What are three current situations (challenging issues) that you are concerned with that we haven't discussed?"
- *Gain information.* "What are the three things your current advisor does not know about your goals, dreams, and legacy?"

- *Improve customer service.* "What are three additional things we could do to strengthen our communication, service, and relationship with you and your family?"

QUESTIONS TO GROW CONTACTS/ RELATIONSHIPS

It is vital that advisors use open-ended questions when networking to broaden their customer base and improve client satisfaction.

- "If there were three things you could spend more time doing with a networking person, what would they be?"
- "If you could spend more time doing three things at a (party, family gathering, networking event), what would they be?"
- "What three activities do you want to engage in at a networking event?"
- "What three follow-up things do you want to do after meeting someone at a networking event?"
- "Tell me a few things you would want a networking person to know about you and how you can help them" or "share with me a few details of what you are looking for in a new client (strategic partner, a person who can help you grow)."

- "What three things do you want to accomplish through networking in the next few years? How will networking help you specifically with your goals?"
- "Share with me some of your biggest networking frustrations. What are some things you can do to improve that situation?"
- "What are a few fun successes you have had with networking? What did they mean to you and how did you feel about them?"

WHAT'S NEXT?

Once a person responds, put the *total listening process* into action.

1. Allow others to speak *without a response.* Leave this until later in the conversation. Focus on them and give the speaker consideration, respect, and the opportunity to empty their bucket.

2. Don't prejudge or make premature comments. Be objective, open and willing to hear *what they are saying rather than what you want or expect to hear.*

3. Then *reflect.* Paraphrase, but don't parrot the speaker, "It sounds like," "it seems that," or "I am hearing that you feel." Make sure what the speaker told you is what you heard and that you understand them.

4. *Clarify.* "Tell me more. Can you further explain? Describe more about that."

5. *Empathize.* "You are not alone. We see that all the time. This happens to many people like yourself."

6. Silence is okay. Reflect and take a break instead of just talking for the purpose of talking.

7. Get the speaker to offer their thoughts or opinions before advising them.

8. Close with a constructive, helpful response. "It seems to me after hearing what you are sharing that," or "we find that with people in this situation," or "what strategies can be done include."

HOW ADVISORS CAN SHOW THEY ARE LISTENING

As advisors, we want clients to like us, accept our advice, and recognize that we are helpful and dedicated to their success. To accomplish that, we must improve our skills and become better listeners. When we listen unconditionally, raise good questions to bring out more from our clients, and allow them to empty their buckets, we bring out our best advisory "hat" because we know what is going on.

In all conversations with customers, avoid distractions, smile, don't speak unless the client asks something, maintain good body language and eye contact, keep engaged, and use cues to encourage the speaker to give more information.

Questioning is an effective way to demonstrate we are listening. We can show we have been paying attention and are interested by asking relevant questions and making reflections that build or make clear what a client has said (Scholtens).[73] Ask, probing, open-ended questions. This shows that you are listening and care about what clients say.

Reflect their responses, "I am hearing you say," "what I understand from your comments is," "what it sounds like," "what I'm getting from you," "would it be accurate to say?" "So you feel that" or "So you are trying to say that?" Pause, then *clarify*, "Okay, go ahead. I'm listening. Keep going. Tell me more. Help me understand." Finally, add *empathy*, "I know how you feel. Many others are facing that same issue."

Only at this point *slowly* share your thoughts. Find a place to summarize the whole situation and see if any things remain to be discussed.

TAKEAWAYS

- As a first step, make the decision that you want to listen.

- Listen in a strict "no judgment zone." Force yourself to enter *every* conversation with an open mind. It is easy to begin a conversation with preconceived ideas about the speaker or their message. Give them a chance to surprise you.

- Make sure you can really hear the other person. Give your *full* attention to them and suspend all other activities. If you multitask while listening, you are *not* listening.

- Use an 80/20 ratio of listening to speaking.

- Unless you are a guest speaker, allow the other party to speak more than you do.

- Be actively interested in what others have to say. Lean toward them, keep good eye contact, and give reassurance messages such as "sounds good," "tell me more," and "that's interesting." By incorporating both verbal and nonverbal responses such as nodding and smiling, others feel more engaged and at ease.

- Don't interrupt the speaker or finish their statements. Let them complete the points they are sharing or wait for a clear pause. Only then, advise, give input, and share your own ideas and opinions.

- Respect those you are advising by empathizing with them, acknowledging their views, and communicating with understanding, patience, and compassion.

CHAPTER 13

DEALING WITH POOR LISTENERS

*"Change happens by listening and then starting
a dialogue with the people who are doing
something you don't believe is right."*
Jane Goodall

Business meetings are notorious places for poor listening and communication breakdowns. Listening is a skill. It takes practice to be a patient, understanding, empathic listener. Before getting upset with poor communication, make sure your own listening behaviors are not the cause.

Stop daydreaming and focus on other speakers, mirror their body language, and use a calm, accepting tone when asking questions. If a point is unclear, repeat it to confirm your understanding. Never make pre-judgments and try to put yourself in the speaker's shoes. Summarize at the end of a conversation to ensure you have fully understood the speaker's message.

You may become aggravated with a rambling, repetitive speaker in the workplace. Sometimes, however, this reaction is caused by your own preconceptions. You know that person never gets to the point, so you immediately tune out as soon as they start talking. As a result, you don't hear a single thing they say.

But what if you are not the cause? Then, you may shorten your agenda to help this type of speaker get to the point or, because you don't want to minimize or cut off the details, sometimes you may allot that person a little more time versus your own capacity to listen comfortably without speaking. Although your personality may not allow for this naturally, you can adapt or "internally compromise" for the betterment of the conversation.

When we are the speakers, listeners may want us to get to the point for a variety of reasons. Some don't want the details because they don't have the time, focus, patience, skill, or experience to listen. The personality of others does not allow them to listen for a long period.

During conversations, these people can be distracted, impatient, or bored. They often miss verbal cues or show their impatience with nonverbal behaviors.

Look around your work environment the next time you are in the board room, with your team, or with others in your work area. Are you all actively communicating with each other? To encourage collaboration and productivity, begin with yourself. Listen more to others, allow them to share and be a part of the conversation. As we want to get people to return to the physical workplace after COVID, we need to make that work environment positive and engaging for everyone.

Not everybody likes to give or get information the same way, and this is also true with bosses. Many supervisors, especially those who seem impatient, want speakers to be brief and to the point without much emotion. If you begin by giving this type of boss the bottom line and a big picture view to gain their buy-in, you've got a good shot at presenting the details of a proposal. But if you prefer process-driven, detailed communications and start with a point "a to z" analysis, such bosses will take a call or tune you out long before they hear your pitch.

To reach this type of supervisor, you must *flex* your speaking style. *Flexing* is not about how you prefer to communicate or how you'd like to have things communicated to you. It's about flexing, or adjusting, your style to that of the boss. This reduces tension and makes the boss more receptive. In this case, what you want to do is to get right to the endpoint and cut to the chase.

Such a direct, concise, and brief style ends impatient behavior, builds a supervisor's trust in you, displays your competence in delivering the results he or she wants, and allows you to grow a fruitful and successful relationship with the boss.

WHAT THE EXPERTS SAY

According to Sabina Nawaz, a global CEO and executive coach:

> Dealing with colleagues who don't listen is both hard and frustrating. When someone is not fully present, it erodes the quality of what you say. The experience might cause you to lose your train of thought or suppress what you originally planned to communicate…. You could [also] get derailed into the drama of why it's happening…. You might take it personally and think, *My colleague is so arrogant.*[74]

According to Christine Riordan, president of Adelphi University and a leadership coach, potential problems aren't limited to hard feelings and misunderstandings. A colleague who doesn't listen can also cause mistakes from an operational standpoint because projects are not correctly executed.

She suggests highlighting the significance of critical points with a phrase like, "I have something important to say and I need you to listen," and emphasizing the importance of the message with an introduction like, "I have something really important to talk to you about, and I need your help" (Riordan).[75] This signals others to stop talking and listen more carefully.

During a conversation, Riordan recommends restating points multiple times in various ways, with statements like, "I want to repeat this, because I want to make sure it's understood," and then, following up with, "Does that make sense?" to ensure others have understood what you said.

Riordan also advises speakers to explicitly state their priorities. If you're dealing with a coworker who tends to *forget* certain conversations, set timelines to anchor your expectations in his mind. Explain that a task is critical for the project and ask for a date when it will be finished. Nawaz agrees that it is important to hold others accountable for listening. When talking to a distracted boss, for example, she suggests letting him or her know you need a "deliverable" by the end of the conversation with a comment like, "I have three strategies that I want to tell you about. In the end, I'm looking for you to decide on one of them."

WHEN OTHERS DON'T LISTEN

Although you can try to improve your own listening habits, you cannot control what others think or do. It's challenging to work with peers, subordinates, or bosses who just don't listen (Knight). Whether they interrupt, ramble, seem distracted, or are always waiting for their turn to talk, the impact is the same: you don't feel heard, and the chances for misunderstandings and mistakes increase.

A poor listener can make you lose confidence in your conversation skills but only if you allow this to happen (Riordan)[76]. It's important to remember that you may not be aware of the issues challenging this listener. However, in the case of repeat offenders or someone who should be listening such as the person who initiated the conversation, it is appropriate to politely acknowledge that you aren't receiving the attention you deserve. After all, everyone wishes to be heard, acknowledged, and respected.

If you think that possibly someone isn't listening, you can attempt to make your conversation more entertaining or change the subject. But you'll *know* someone isn't listening when they interrupt you in mid-sentence, look away as you speak, look at you but fail to acknowledge anything that you've said, change subjects with no transition, interrupt, argue with you about things you didn't say, or take what you did say out of context.

ENCOURAGE OTHERS TO LISTEN

Rather than angrily watching every annoying thing this person does, take action to encourage them to listen. As a first step, decide that you don't want this moment to pass without disclosing that you have noticed, although you value the listener and your communication with them, that they do not appear to be listening to you. If it is necessary to point out poor listening behaviors, try to do it in a positive, compassionate way.

Make a statement like, "John, you and I can talk to each other courteously, but it doesn't seem to me that right now you are hearing what I'm saying," or "Chris, I care about you but right now I'm getting signals from you that indicate you aren't hearing what I'm saying. Would you mind highlighting what you think I'm talking about and then give me time to respond?"

Another tactic you can use is a probing question such as, "You seem distracted. Is there anything I can help you with?" (Knight)[77] You might also test listening behaviors with statements like, "Tell me what you understood about what I said" or "you just heard me explain what was important to me. Please share and review what I just said to you." Requesting a recap of your communication is a highly effective tool for both advisors and clients, especially when interviewing.

Following are additional strategies for collaborating with colleagues who never seem to listen (Knight).[78]

- Consider their work styles and ask how they like to receive information. Some people are visual while others are verbal.
- Discover something of personal interest to the other person that they enjoy discussing.
- If you find your conversation is getting heated, let the speaker know that you prefer to talk later when both of you can be civil in tone. "When's a good time for you?" During this "break" from the conversation, forgive the other person for any offense you may have felt.
- Acknowledge, respond, and encourage the conversation along by saying, "Tell me more about." Be an empathic listener. Let your colleagues say what they need to. When the conversation reaches a natural pause, validate their points, and then share your thoughts.

CHAPTER 14

LISTENING BENEFITS IN EVERYDAY LIFE

"It takes a good man [or woman] to be a good listener."
Calvin Coolidge

Great listening requires empathy, patience, reflection, clarification, self-control, respect, understanding, and consideration. To become an outstanding listener, you must intentionally develop and practice your skills until the total listening process becomes a habit. Good listeners have a much better awareness of what others are thinking beyond the surface. That's true in all relationships — business, personal, family, and common social interactions.

AN EASY EXERCISE TO IMPROVE LISTENING SKILLS

One of the best ways to become a better listener is to practice (Osten).[79] The following exercise takes only four minutes, but it helps you understand how active listening feels so that you can put it into action in your everyday encounters:

Find a willing participant. Then face each other with no distractions other than a watch or a timer ("Are You Really Listening, or Just Waiting to Talk?"). For two minutes, one of you answers the prompt, "How are you?" while the other listens. If you are the listener, *make no verbal responses* during that time. You may use facial expressions or nod your head. Listen to the speaker's words for the sake of listening, not for the sake of replying. Then, switch roles for the last two minutes (Osten).[80]

LISTENING TO RESPOND VERSUS UNDERSTAND

Listening behaviors impact every aspect of our lives. We listen (or don't) during meetings, conflict situations, and in everyday conversations with bosses, coworkers, subordinates, parents, kids, friends, and spouses. As introduced in Chapter 2, we often listen to respond rather than to understand, and we are sometimes not even consciously aware of how we are listening (Osten).[81] To identify your listening mode during a given exchange, intentionally observe your thoughts, attitude, and body language. For example, while your friend was talking about his vacation, you gathered your thoughts about your own trip so that you could immediately reply with how great it was.

Listening to respond is often competitive or judgmental. Your mind wanders to other thoughts while you impatiently wait to speak. You may be restless and tap your fingers or feet. Your body language conveys your apathy and indifference to the ideas of others. When another person wants some acknowledgement or clarification, you do not provide it because anything you say might be used to debate your position.

When *listening to understand*, you suspend judgment. You catch yourself when your thoughts stray and bring your focus back to the conversation. You ask for clarification. You empathize. You are able to separate facts and their interpretation (feelings), and respect both without discounting either. You understand the words, but also try to understand the feelings behind those words. You listen not just to what is said, but also to what is unsaid.

We all want others to understand us and know what we are feeling, but communication is a two-way street. Listening to someone else makes them trust, feel comfortable, and want to share with you. When you add listening to trust, comfort, and empathy, you create strong and enduring relationships.

"One way to be a better listener is to *ask questions of others*" (Plante).[82] Using more questions to understand rather than respond in your conversations forces you to talk less and helps improve your listening skills. For example, if your spouse asks you to pick up eggs on the way home, make sure you know what he or she really wants. Ask, "Large, extra-large, or organic? Any special brand?" and don't bring milk instead.

This will help you grow emotionally stronger, deepen your perception of others' feelings, and promote engagement, trust, and comfort in your communications. Only then will you truly hear and fully realize what speakers are feeling and talking about. With this increased clarity, your responses will become more thorough and meaningful, and have a greater impact. You will ask better questions that reveal speakers' underlying issues, and they will open up, share, and trust you more.

How many times have you found yourself in a circle of friends competing for speaking space or the ability to display your extensive knowledge as opposed to balancing the amount of time you stay quiet? You should first figure out if you want to speak and what your comments will contribute, or if you would prefer just to listen. "A good listener is someone who doesn't in some way end up turning the conversation around to himself" (Kaplowitz).[83]

Good listening during everyday interactions is important for many reasons. There's the obvious practical side - you can't do well academically if you don't pay attention to instructions, you'll get in trouble at home if you drown out your spouse's concerns, and you won't keep a job if you ignore your boss.

Being a good listener also broadens your perspective and makes you a more approachable person (Cruse).[84] As you present yourself as patient and caring, people naturally feel more inclined to communicate with you. There are many people in this world who fervently wish to have at least a single friend who can "listen." By being there for them, you give them the freedom to express their feelings. As Stephen Covey put it, "You give them psychological air and end their mental suffocation."

THE PERSONAL BENEFITS

Improving your listening skills results in better, more meaningful dialogue, stronger relationships based on deeper appreciation and respect for others, and a clearer understanding of the details in conversations. According to writer Roxanna Coldiron, "The benefits to becoming a better listener are longer, stronger friendships, fewer arguments, and more insight" (Coldiron).[85] Learning to listen will help you to understand and empathize with others and that will also improve your intuition.

Total listening will deepen and strengthen your relationships with friends and family as you become a better, more effective, and stronger communicator. Take, for instance, speaking with children. My daughter is a good communicator and a great debater with strong opinions. She has an amazing wit, and her sarcasm can be a great challenge to my parental pontification and exaggerated claims of knowledge.

Like many families, we frequently cut each other off and interrupt while the other person is still speaking. She starts telling me something and I jump in and say, "Oh you mean" or "Oh yeah, I know." Then she looks at me and says, "That's not what I was going to say," or "that's not what I'm talking about," or even makes the killer comment, "Do you want to tell me what I'm trying to tell you, or do you want to let me finish?" That is a sure sign I'm *not* listening!

Effective listening will help you understand the needs of those around you and will produce more harmonious and lasting relationships. "You can make more friends in two months by being interested in them than you can in two years by making them interested in you" (Carnegie). Those same listening skills will not only be appreciated by others and make you more popular company, but you may hear novel points of view, different perspectives, and gain new insights. You may even get some good advice.

Listening will help you develop more patience and tolerance, as well as help you solve problems and see new opportunities (Schwantes).[86]

IMPROVED HAPPINESS THROUGH TOTAL LISTENING

When you apply the total listening process to everyday life, both you and those around you become happier people. Smiling is contagious. Send a note, text, or email to someone with an open-ended question and then listen to the response. Pick up the phone and call someone to say, "Hi. What's going on with you?" Then listen with 100% attention. Pay a compliment to a friend and try to get them to share more, "I love your hair! How did you find such a lovely cut?" or, "that's a chic outfit. I'd love to hear all about it." Then listen.

Forgive someone else or apologize, ask how they feel about what you just shared, and listen to their reply. Hug, high five, or fist pump someone. Ask them how they got to be such a great person, then listen to their response. Open a conversation with, "I love (like, care about) you. I just wanted you to know. I hope you're okay with that. Any thoughts?" And listen.

Listen more and talk less. Reflect more and go deeper. Stay positive and good things will happen. How do you expand the world of listening to life lessons and translate that into a legacy of things that are really important to you? To truly further relationships and make interactions, exchanges, dialogues, and discussions more beneficial, become a better listener. Others will appreciate that, appreciate you more, and you will be happier as a result.

CHAPTER 15

CONCLUSION AND ACTION STEPS

*"I remind myself every morning: Nothing I
say this day will teach me anything. So, if I'm
going to learn, I must do it by listening."*
Larry King

CONCLUSION

Great listeners fully understand what others want to say
and accurately simplify complex verbal messages. Like
the television detective Columbo, they ask probing questions. On every episode just before he solved the crime,
he would pause as he was leaving, turn around, and say
the famous line, "One last question." He'd let the perpe-
trator talk, and *boom!* the crime was solved.

We must listen to a wide range of people each day. Co-workers, bosses, parents, kids, friends, teachers, coaches, mentors, significant others, and new acquaintances speak to us at meetings; on the job; at our places of worship, at the kids' schools, sports, and activities; on the street; in our homes; and during community gatherings.

Approach each of these many conversations with the intent to learn something. It's awfully hard to learn anything while you are talking.

Strive to talk less and think more about what you are learning. As so appropriately said by Mark Twain, the pseudonym of writer Samuel Clemens, "If we were meant to talk more than listen, we would have two mouths and one ear."[87] Instead of focusing on what you are going to say next, it is often helpful to repeat what the speaker is saying in your mind.

Wayne Gretzky is renowned as a top hockey player. A reporter once asked, "What is your secret? What makes you one of the greatest of all time?" Gretzky mentioned that fellow hockey greats all shot with incredible accuracy and got to the puck quickly but then shared the one thing which differentiated him from the others. Gretzky said, "I skate to where the puck is going to be, not to where it has been."

This is also true with listening. Remember this the next time you are in a challenging conversation, a heated debate, or a high-energy, intense exchange. If we don't interrupt and get the speaker to go deeper, we are listening to understand and getting to the more meaningful and impactful place that the conversation will be going next.

QUICK REVIEW OF LISTENING TIPS

- When listening, always think, *What can I learn from this conversation?*
- Ask open-ended questions like, "What did you feel?" or "how did you deal with that?"
- Have the speaker share a story or example, then respond with what you learned or what surprised you most about that situation.
- Don't immediately prepare a response. Before you reply, take in all the comments, tone, information, and message of the speaker.
- Keep your body language, including facial expressions, caring, attentive, and respectful. Lean toward the speaker.
- Maintain eye contact but remember not to stare or stand so close that you break into the speaker's space or safe zone.
- Silence is not necessarily bad. Sometimes it creates time to pause, reflect, and gather your thoughts.

- Try not to fidget. Don't tap your fingers, cross your arms, or keep looking at your watch.
- Look at the speaker rather than at your phone during conversations.
- Nod to acknowledge the statements of others, maintain good posture, and share similar body language to that of the speaker.
- Try to include inflection while speaking. Change your tone, delivery speed, and smile when appropriate.
- Reflect by repeating or paraphrasing what the speaker has said. Summarize at the end to ensure a clear understanding of their message and concerns.
- Give others time to respond. Try not to rush or hurry them. Be patient. Let the speaker finish before you speak. You are not the only one with something to share.

RECAP OF STEPS IN TOTAL LISTENING

Total listening allows clients to realize that you are truly in their corner and ready to help them achieve their goals and aspirations.

Begin by *attending*. Remove distractions from both you and the speaker. Then, *reflect* client concerns, issues, obstacles, or objections. Make sure to clearly understand with statements such as, "The issue seems to be," "it sounds like," or "you're feeling as if."

When the speaker confirms, don't respond. Instead, ask them to *clarify*. "Tell me more about that," or "can you give more detail on that issue?" or "help me understand that challenge more." Let them talk, empty their bucket, and share a deeper explanation. Don't cut them off. Truly listen to their response.

Next, *empathize* by saying, "That's quite common. We've seen that many times. You aren't alone in that concern. Many others feel the same way." Such nonjudgmental comments confirm that you have seen, heard, and experienced what the speaker is feeling and understand what they are going through.

Then ask if the speaker has additional concerns, "Now that we've talked about that issue, what are some other concerns, thoughts and things on your mind?" This allows speakers to fully empty their bucket and share everything that is important to them. Only at this point, respond with compassion, patience, and credibility to offer your amazing skill set, expertise, direction, and advice.

THINGS TO DO AFTER YOU HAVE READ THIS BOOK

- Set a goal for active and reflective listening.
- Keep a log of your conversations and evaluate their components. Did the conversation go well? Did you reflect? Did you actively engage and listen without distraction? Did you clarify and give the person a chance to empty their bucket?
- Review one or two ways to improve your conversations each week.
- Create a workbook of your successes highlighting improvements in the way you listen and how that has strengthened a business or personal relationship.

Congratulations on completing this book. Now is the exciting time to become a total better listener. I am confident that with some practice and implementation of the action steps, you will see an absolute difference and improvement in both your professional and personal life—and that is why we have two ears and one mouth.

GOOD LUCK! I would love to hear from you. Email your thoughts or results to me at betterlisteningbook@gmail.com.

THANK YOU
FOR READING

For discounted bulk purchases of this book for your company, association, or conference, please email us at **betterlisteningbook@gmail.com**

To book Stanford Slovin for interviews or speaking, visit **www.betterlisteningbook.com** or contact **betterlisteningbook@gmail.com**

ABOUT THE AUTHOR

For over thirty years, Stanford Slovin has worked in the securities industry with individuals, families, and business owners as a financial professional with major national brokerage firms. Stan  earned his Bachelor of Science degree in finance at the Champaign-Urbana campus of the University of Illinois. He also holds a Juris Doctorate from the University of Illinois Chicago School of Law. Stan is actively involved in charitable organizations focusing on mental health and children with disabilities. He loves traveling and plays in a rock 'n' roll band. Stan, his wife, and their two adult children are from the Chicagoland area.

REFERENCES

Arcieri, James. "Leadership Series #4: Great Leaders Are Great Listeners." *Linkedin*, 21 Nov 2020, www.linkedin .com/pulse/ leadership-series-4-great-leaders-listeners-james-arcieri#:~:text=James%20Arcieri,- Head%20 of%20Strategic&text=Great%20 leaders%20are%20 great%20listeners%2C%20and%20therefore%20 my%20message%20today,by% 20talking%2C%20 but%20 by%20listening.

"The Benefits of Good Communication in Accounting." *Hubstaff Blog*, 2022, blog. hubstaff.com/accounting-communication/.

Bhasin, Hitesh. "Empathic Listening: Definition, Qualities, Skills and Tips." *Marketing91*, 16 Oct 2020, www.marketing91.com/empathic- listening/.

Billows, Rochelle. "Want Your Marriage to Last?" *YourTango.com*, 18 Nov 2013, *www.yourtango.com/experts/rochelle- bilow/want-your-marriage-last#hide.*

Blount, Jeb. *Sales EQ: How Ultra High Performers Leverage Sales – Specific Emotional Intelligence to Close the Complex Deal.* John Wiley & Sons Inc., 2017.

Buscaglia, Leo. "Please Listen." Quoted by Christina Beck in "Listen to Me!" *Supportiv*, 16 Dec 2021, www.supportiv.com/stress- relief/listen-to-me.

Carnegie, Dale. *The Leader In You*. Simon and Schuster, p41, 2012.

Coldiron, Roxanna. "How to Become a Better Listener." *Yahoo! Living*, 14 Sep 2020, www.yahoo.com/now/become-better- listener-130021185.html.

Collins, James C. *Good to Great (Why Some Companies Make the Leap…and Others Don't)*. Harper, 1958. Audio, 2001.

Covey, Stephen R. *The 7 Habits of Highly Effective People.* Simon & Schuster, 19 May 2020.

Cruse, Rose. "It Is Important to Be a Better Listener. Why?" *Medium*, 16 Oct 2017, medium.com/@ cruserose95/it-is-important- to-be-a-good-listener-why- 8823ffb8651d.

Doyle, Allison. "What Are Listening Skills?" *The Balance Careers,* 7 Jul 2022, www.thebalancecareers. com/types-of- listening-skills-with-examples-2063759.

Eades, John G. *Building the Best: 8 Proven Leadership Principles to Elevate Others to Success.* McGraw-Hill, 2020.

"Effective Listening and How to Be a Better Listener." *MastersinCommunication*, 2022, mastersincommunications.org/effective- listening/.

El, Sa. "How Many People Die from Texting and Driving? 81+ Distracted Driving Statistics." *Simply Insurance*, 11 Jan 2022, www.simplyinsurance.com/ texting-and- driving-statistics/.

"Empathic Listening." *Mind Tools*, Emerald Works, 2022, www.mindtools.com/ a8l9j08/empathic-listening.

"English Club." ЗНО від Н.П.Сергієнко: 1cop!, 2014, englishvpunszno.blogspot.com/2014/ 11/girls-of- group-1cop.html.

"Enhancing Your Listening." *Boundless Communications*, Course Hero, 2022, www.coursehero.com/file/ 24331509/ Improving-Your-Listening-Skillsdocx/.

"Epictetus Quotes." *BrainyQuote.com*, BrainyMedia Inc., 2022, www.brainyquote. com/quotes/epictetus_ 10622298.

Folkman, Joe and Zengler, Jack. "What Great Leaders Actually Do." *Harvard Business Review*, 14 Jul 2016, hbr.org/2016/07/ what-great-listeners-actually-do.

Freese, Thomas A. *Secrets of Question-Based Selling,* 2nd Edition. Sourcebooks, 2013.

Gardner, Howard. *Changing Minds: The Art and Science of Changing Our Own and Other People's Minds (Leadership for the Common Good).* Harvard Business Review Press, 2016.

Goodall, Jane. Quoted in "63 Inspirational Quotes on Active Listening." *Gracious Quotes*, 9 Aug 2022, www. graciousquotes.com/ active-listening/.

Gray, John. *Men Are from Mars, Women Are from Venus: A Practical Guide for Improving Communication and Getting What You Want in Your Relationships.* Harper Collins, 1992.

Harris, Thomas R. "6 Poor Listening Habits that Can Hurt Our Relationships." *The Exceptional Skills*, Radiant Hope, LLC., 28 Aug 2020, www.theexceptionalskills. com/6-poor- listening-habits-can-hurt-relationships/.

"How Listening Can Help Improve Client Relationships in Accounting." *Becker CPA Review*, 12 Jan 2016, www.wscpa.org/ community/future-cpas/ become-a-cpa- blog/wscpa-blog/2016/01/12/how- listening- can-help-improve-client-relationships-in- accounting#. YwlBhXbMK3A.

"Investor Expectations A New Survey." *Vanguard Research*, Feb 2020, corporate. vanguard.com/content/ dam/corp/ research/pdf/investor-expectations-a-new- survey-us-isgies_022020_online.pdf.

Jackson, Dean. Quoted in "Listening." *AMS Blogs,* American Mathematical Society, 25 Nov 2019, blogs. ams.org/phdplus/2019/ 11/25/listening/.

Kaplowitz, Stuart. "What does It Mean to Be a Good Listener?" *Good Therapy*, 22 Jul 2013, www. goodtherapy.org/blog/what-does-it- mean-to-be-good- listener-0722136#:-:text= Being%20a%20good% 20listener%20is,ask%20questions %2C%20and %20 offer%20support.

Katz, Neil and McNulty, Kevin. *Reflexive Listening*, pdf., 1994, www.maxwell.syr.edu/ docs/default-source/ ektron-files/reflective- listening-nk.pdf?sfvrsn=f1fa6672_5.

King, Larry. Quoted in "63 Inspirational Quotes on Active Listening." *Gracious Quotes,* 9 Aug 2022, www. graciousquotes.com/active- listening/.

Knight, Rebecca. "How to Work with a Bad Listener." *Harvard Business Review,* 24 Aug 2017, hbr.org/2017/ 08/how-to-work-with-a- bad-listener.

Llopis, Glenn. "6 Ways Effective Listening Can Make You a Better Leader." *Forbes,* 20 May 2013, Forbes. com/sites/glennllopis/2013/ 05/20/6-effective-ways- listening-can-make- you-a-better-leader/? sh= 2f8c2da51756.

McCumber, Alyssa. Quoted in "63 Inspirational Quotes on Active Listening." *Gracious Quotes,* 9 Aug 2022, www.graciousquotes.com/ active-listening/.

Nichols, Ralph. Quoted in "63 Inspirational Quotes on Active Listening." *Gracious Quotes,* 9 Aug 2022, www. graciousquotes.com/ active-listening/.

Nulty, Peter. Quoted in "Quotes About Listening." *Leading Thoughts,* LeadershipNow, 2019, www. leadershipnow. com/listeningquotes.html.

Obama, Barack. "Xavier University Commencement Address." New Orleans, Louisiana, 11 Aug 2006.

Orwell, George. *Down and Out in Paris and London*, 1933, reprinted by Harcourt, Brace, 1950.

Osten, Caren. "Are You Really Listening, or Just Waiting to Talk?" *Psychology Today*, 5 Oct 2016, www.psychologytoday.com/us/blog/ the-right-balance/201610/ are-you-really- listening-or-just-waiting-talk.

Palumbo, Dennis. "Getting Out of Your Own Way." Psychology Today, 27 Mar 2013, www.psychologytoday.com/us/blog/ hollywood-on-the-couch/201303/ getting- out-of-your-own-way.

Plante, Thomas G. "Three Ways to Be a Better Listener." *Psychology Today*, 22 Sep 2014, www.psychologytoday.com/us/blog/do-the- right-thing/201409/three-ways-be-better- listener.

"Richard Branson Biography." *The Biography.com*, A&E Television, 3 Apr 2018, www.biography.com/business-figure/ richard-branson.

Ridgely, D. Quoted in "63 Inspirational Quotes on Active Listening." *Gracious Quotes,* 9 Aug 2022, www.graciousquotes.com/active- listening/.

Riordan, Christine. "How to Work with a Bad Listener." *Harvard Business Review*, Aug 2017, p152, hbr.org/2017/08/how-to-work- with-a-bad-listener.

Robbins, Anthony. "Ask Better Questions." *Mind and Meaning*, Robbins Research International, Inc., 2022, www.tonyrobbins. com/mind-meaning/ask-better-questions/.

Roerink, Alide. A Call to Bring the World Together." *Earth Charter*, Earth Charter International, 12 Nov 2009, earthcharter.org/ charter-for-compassion-a-call-to-bring-the- world-together/?gclid= CjwKCAjw6ra YBhB7Eiw ABge5Klhdz7BRH02g5YHujeVbWd JkCrjRN1LYDM U2UnbyOeb_BtXzfLrxDhoCK 18QAvD_BwE.

Rusoff, Jane Wollman. "The 4 Types of Client Objections and How to Meet Them Head-On." *Think Advisor*, 12 Jul 2018, www.thinkadvisor.com/2018/07/ 12/the-4- types-of-client-objections-and-how-to-overcome-them/.

Scholtens, Zach. "Active Listening Flashcards." *Quizlet*, Quizlet, Inc., 2022, quizlet.com/ 105232402/active-listening-skills-flash- cards/#:~:text=What%20is%20 active%20 listening%3F,the%20attention%20on%20 the%20speaker&text=You%20just%20studied% 209%20terms.

Schwantes, Marcel. "5 Surprising Benefits of Being a Great Listener." *Inc.com.*, 16 Oct 2016, www.inc.com/ marcel-schwantes/not- a-good-listener-these-5-immediate- workplace-benefits-may-change-your- mind.html.

Scott, Steve. "3 Tips on How to be Tolerant of Others." *Internet Lifestyle Without the B.S.*, 2014, www. stevescottsite.com/3-tips-on- how-to-be-tolerant-of-others.

Seaton, Holly. "Leaders Listen Up: Better Listening Equals Better Leadership." *Flashpoint Consulting*, 14 Jul 2016, www.flashpointleadership.com/blog/leaders- listen-up-better-listening-equals-better- leadership.

"Self-Disclosure." MindTools, Emerald Works Limited, 2022, www.mindtools.com/agr7y2v/self-disclosure.

Sullivan, Bob and Thompson, Hugh. *The Plateau Effect: Getting from Stuck to Success.* Dutton, Inc., 2013.

"The Ultimate List of Marketing Statistics for 2022." *HubSpot Knowledge Base*, 2022, www.hubspot.com/ marketing-statistics.

"Warm Up: PLEASE LISTEN!" Slide presentation, *Juniper Young*, SlidePlayer.com Inc., 2022, slideplayer. com/slide/4630345/.

"What is NPS? Your Ultimate Guide to Net Promoter." *Qualtrics*, 2022, www.qualtrics. com/experience-management/customer/ net-promoter-score/.

"Why is Listening an Important Soft Skill?" *By Weeknd*, 28 Dec 2021, byweeknd.com/2920157/.

Yugay, Irina. "Empathy vs. Sympathy: Learn to Truly Love and Care." *MindValley*, 17 Feb 2018. blog. mindvalley.com/empathy-vs- sympathy/.

ENDNOTES

1   "What's the Difference Between Hearing and Listening?" *Healthline* online. Last modified September 26, 2018. https://www.healthline.com/health/hearing-vs-listening#takeaway.

2   Eades, John, *Building the Best: 8 Proven Leadership to Elevate Others to Success* (New York: McGraw-Hill, 2019).

3   "Top 350 Andy Stanley Quotes," last modified May 3, 2023, https://quotefancy.com/andy-stanley-quotes.

4   Covey, Stephen R. *The 7 Habits of Highly Effective People.* New York: Simon & Schuster, 1999.

5   Sullivan, Bob, and Hugh Thompson. *Getting Unstuck: Breaking Free of the Plateau Effect.* New York: E.F. Dutton, 2013.

6   Plante, Thomas G. "Three Ways to Be a Better Listener." *Psychology Today* online. Last modified September 22, 2014. https://www.psychologytoday.com/us/blog/do-the-right-thing/201409/three-ways-be-better-listener.

7   Schwantes, Marcel. *5 Surprising Benefits of Being a Great Listener.* Last modified October 6, 2016. https://www.inc.com/marcel-schwantes/not-a-good-listener-these-5-immediate-workplace-benefits-may-change-your-mind.html.

8   Sullivan and Thompson, *Getting Unstuck: Breaking Free of the Plateau Effect.*

9   Sa El. "How Many People Die from Texting and Driving?" Last modified February 4, 2023. https://www.simplyinsurance.com/texting-and-driving-statistics/.

10 Gardner, Howard. *Changing Minds: The Art and Science of Changing Our Own and Other People's Minds (Leadership for the Common Good)*. Brighton, Massachusetts: Harvard Business Review Press, 2006.

11 Katz, Neil and Kevin McNulty. "Reflective Listening." *Syracuse University* PDF online, 1994. https://www.maxwell.syr.edu/docs/default-source/ektron-files/reflective-listening-neil-katz-and-kevin-mcnulty.pdf?sfvrsn=f1fa6672_7.

12 Doyle, Alison. "What Are Listening Skills?" *The Balance* online. Last modified July 7, 2022. https://www.thebalancemoney.com/types-of-listening-skills-with-examples-2063759.

13 Ibid.

14 Osten, Caren. "Are You Really Listening, or Just Waiting to Talk?" *Psychology Today* online. Last modified October 5, 2016. https://www.psychologytoday.com/us/blog/the-right-balance/201610/are-you-really-listening-or-just-waiting-talk.

15 Spears, M.M."Active Listening Skills." Accessed May 5, 2023. https://quizlet.com/105232402/active-listening-skills-flash-cards/#%3A~%3Atext%3DWhat%20is%20active%20%20listening%3F%2Cthe%20attention%20on%20the%20speaker.%26text%3DYou%20just%20studied%209%20terms.

16 Katz and McNulty. "Reflective Listening."

17 Ibid.

18 Osten, "Are You Really Listeening, or Just Waiting to Talk?"

19 Katz and McNulty. "Reflective Listening."

20 Ibid.

21 Ibid.

22 Ibid.

23 Ibid.

24 Ibid.

25 Ibid.

26 Osten, "Are You Really Listening, or Just Waiting to Talk?"

27 Ibid.

28 Robbins, Tony. "Ask Better Questions." Accessed May 5, 2023. https://www.tonyrobbins.com/mind-meaning/ask-better-questions/.

29 Doyle. "What Are Listening Skills?"

30 Obama, Barack. "Xavier University Commencement Address."
    Last modified August 11, 2006. http://obamaspeeches.com/087-
    Xavier-University-Commencement-Address-Obama-Speech.htm.

31 Yugay, Irina. "Empathy vs. Sympathy: Learn to Truly Love and
    Care." Last modified February 17, 2018. https://blog.mindvalley.
    com/empathy-vs-sympathy/.

32 Vankat, S.R. "What Is an Empath?" Last modified November 9,
    2022. https://www.webmd.com/balance/what-is-an-empath.

33 Bhasin, Hitesh. "Empathic Listening: Definition, Qualities,
    Skills and Tips," Last modified October 16, 2020. https://www.
    marketing91.com/empathic-listening/.

34 Ibid.

35 Osten, "Are You Really Listening, or Just Waiting to Talk?"

36 Bhasin. ""Empathic Listening: Definition, Qualities, Skills and
    Tips."

37 Kaplowitz, Stuart A. "What Does It Mean to Be a Good
    Listener?" Last modified July 22, 2013. https://www.
    goodtherapy.org/blog/what-does-it-mean-to-be-good-listener-
    0722136#%3A~%3Atext%3D%20Being%20a%20good%25
    %2020listener%20is%2Cask%20%20questions%20%2C%20
    and%20%20offer%20%20support.

38 Covey. *The 7 Habits of Highly Effective People.*

39 Scott, Steve. "3 Tips on How to Be Tolerant of Others." Last
    modified October 30, 2010. https://www.stevescottsite.com/3-
    tips-on-how-to-be-tolerant-of-others.

40 Bhasin. ""Empathic Listening: Definition, Qualities, Skills and
    Tips."

41 Ibid.

42 Blount, Jeb. *Sales EQ: How Ultra High Performers Leverage
    Sales-Specific Emotional Intelligence to Close the Complex Deal.*
    Hoboken, New Jersey: John Wiley & Sons, Inc., 2017.

43 Ibid.

44 Ibid.

45 Rusoff, Jane Wollman. "The 4 Types of Client Objections and
    How to Meet Them Head-On." Last modified July 12, 2018.
    https://www.thinkadvisor.com/2018/07/12/the-4-types-of-client-
    objections-and-how-to-overcome-them/.

46 Blount, Jeb. "Activating the Self Disclosure Loop." *Sales Gravy.*
    Accessed May 5, 2023. Podcast, MP3 audio, 5:15. https://
    salesgravy.com/activating-the-self-disclosure-loop-podcast/.

47 Plante. "Three Ways to Be a Better Listener."

48 Russoff. "The 4 Types of Client Objections and How to Meet Them Head-On."

49 Bilow, Rochelle. "What Your Marriage to Last?" Last modified November 18, 2013. https://www.yourtango.com/experts/rochelle-bilow/want-your-marriage-last.

50 Ibid.

51 Gray, John. *Men Are from Mars, Women Are from Venus: A Practical Guide for Improving Communication and Getting What You Want in Your Relationships.* New York: Harper Collins, 1992.

52 "The Ultimate List of Marketing Statistics for 2022." HubSpot. Accessed May 5, 2023. https://www.hubspot.com/marketing-statistics.

53 "What Is NPS? Your Ultimate Guide to Net Promoter." Qualtrics. Accessed May 5, 2023. https://www.qualtrics.com/experience-management/customer/net-promoter-score/.

54 Folkman, Joe and Jack Zengler. "What Great Leaders Actually Do." Last modified July 14, 2016. https://hbr.org/2016/07/what-great-listeners-actually-do.

56 Schwantes, Marcel. "5 Surprising Benefits of Being a Great Listener." Last modified October 6, 2016. https://www.inc.com/marcel-schwantes/not-a-good-listener-these-5-immediate-workplace-benefits-may-change-your-mind.html.

57 Cruse, Rose. "It Is Important to Be a Better Listener. Why?" Last modified October 17, 2017. https://medium.com/@cruserose95/it-is-important-to-be-a-good-listener-why-8823ffb8651d.

58 Plante, Thomas G. "Three Ways to Be a Better Listener." Last modified September 22, 2014. https://www.psychologytoday.com/us/blog/do-the-right-thing/201409/three-ways-be-better-listener.

59

60 Osten. "Are You Really Listening, or Just Waiting to Talk?"

61 Schwantes, Marcel. *5 Surprising Benefits of Being a Great Listener.*

62 Welker, Bruce. "The Benefits of Good Communication in Accounting and How to Do It Well." Last modified July 10, 2019. https://blog.hubstaff.com/accounting-communication/.

63 "How Listening Can Help Improve Client Relationships in Accounting." *Washington Society of Certified Public Accountants* online. January 12, 2016. https://www.wscpa.org/community/future-cpas/become-a-cpa-blog/wscpa-blog/2016/01/12/how-listening-can-help-improve-client-relationships-in-accounting#.ZFhvIc7MKUk.

64 Schwantes, Marcel. "5 Surprising Benefits of Being a Great Listener."

65 Young, Juniper. "Warm Up: PLEASE LISTEN!" *SlidePlayer* online. Accessed May 6, 2023. Slide show, 2:42. https://slideplayer.com/slide/4630345/.

66 Llopis, Glenn. "6 Ways Effective Listening Can Make You a Better Leader." *Forbes* online. Last modified May 20, 2013. https://www.forbes.com/sites/glennllopis/2013/05/20/6-effective-ways-listening-can-make-you-a-better-leader/?sh=60749d0f1756. 05/20/6-effective-ways-listening-can-make- you-a-better-leader/? sh=2f8c2da51756.

67 Arcieri, James. "Leadership Series #4: Great Leaders are Great Listeners." Last modified November 21, 2020. https://www.linkedin.com/pulse/leadership-series-4-great-leaders-listeners-james-arcieri.

68 Ibid.

69 Seaton, Holly. "Leaders Listen Up: Better Listening Equals Better Leadership." Last modified July 14, 2016. https://www.flashpointleadership.com/blog/leaders-listen-up-better-listening-equals-better-leadership.

70 Ibid.

71 Osten. "Are You Really Listening, or Just Waiting to Talk?"

72 "Richard Branson Biography." *Biography* online. Last modified November 2, 2021. https://www.biography.com/business-leaders/richard-branson.

73 Spears, M.M."Active Listening Skills."

74 Nawaz, Sabina. "How to Work with a Bad Listener." Quoted in article by Rebecca Knight. Last modified August 24, 2017. https://hbr.org/2017/08/how-to-work-with-a-bad-listener.

75 Riordan, Christine. "How to Work with a Bad Listener." Quoted in article by Rebecca Knight. Last modified August 24, 2017. https://hbr.org/2017/08/how-to-work-with-a-bad-listener.

76 Ibid.

77 Knight, Rebecca. "How to Work with a Bad Listener." Last modified August 24, 2017. https://hbr.org/2017/08/how-to-work-with-a-bad-listener

78 Ibid.

79 Osten. "Are You Really Listening, or Just Waiting to Talk?"

80 Ibid.

81 Ibid.

82 Plante, Thomas G. "Three Ways to Be a Better Listener."

83   Kaplowitz, Stuart. "What Does It Mean to Be a Good
     Listener?" Last modified July 22, 2013. https://www.
     goodtherapy.org/blog/what-does-it-mean-to-be-good-
     listener-0722136#%3A~%3Atext%3D%20Being%20a%20
     good%25%2020listener%20is%2Cask%20%20questions%20
     %2C%20and%20%20offer%20%20support.

84   Rose Cruse. "It Is Important to Be a Better Listener. Why?" Last
     modified October 16, 2017. medium.com/@cruserose95/it-is-
     important- to-be-a-good-listener-why-8823ffb8651d.

85   Roxanna Coldiron. "How to Become a Better Listener." Last
     modified September 14, 2020. https://www.yahoo.com/lifestyle/
     become-better-listener-130021185.html.

86   Schwantes, Marcel. "5 Surprising Benefits of Being a Great
     Listener."

87   This quote is commonly attributed to Mark Twain, but the
     original source remains unclear.